SO, YOU WANT

To Be a

DANCER?

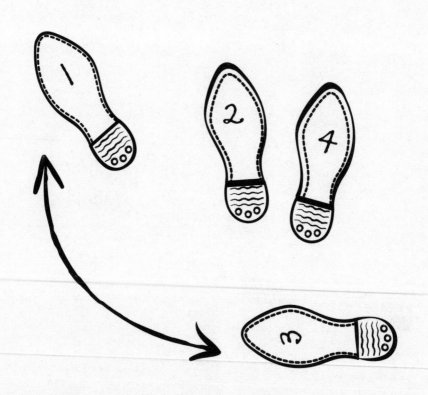

SO, YOU WANT To Be a DANCER?

The Ultimate Guide to Exploring the DANCE INDUSTRY

Laurel van der Linde

BE WHAT YOU WANT Series

ALADDIN
New York London Toronto Sydney New Delhi

BEYOND WORDS
Hillsboro, Oregon

ALADDIN
An imprint of Simon & Schuster
Children's Publishing Division
1230 Avenue of the Americas
New York, NY 10020

BEYOND WORDS
20827 N.W. Cornell Road, Suite 500
Hillsboro, Oregon 97124-9808
503-531-8700 / 503-531-8773 fax
www.beyondword.com

For information about special discounts for bulk purchases, please contact
Simon & Schuster Special Sales at 1-866-506-1949 or business@simonandschuster.com.

The Simon & Schuster Speakers Bureau can bring authors to your live event.
For more information or to book an event contact the Simon & Schuster Speakers
Bureau at 1-866-248-3049 or visit our website at www.simonspeakers.com.

Managing Editor: Lindsay S. Brown
Editors: Kristin Thiel, Emmalisa Sparrow
Proofreader: Jen Weaver-Neist
Design: Sara E. Blum
The text of this book was set in Bembo and Interstate.

Manufactured in the United States of America 0315 FFG

10 9 8 7 6 5 4 3 2 1

Library of Congress Cataloging-in-Publication Data

Van der Linde, Laurel
    So, you want to be a dancer? : the ultimate guide to exploring the dance industry /
    Laurel van der Linde.
    pages   cm. — (Be what you want series)
    Includes bibliographical references.
    1. Dance—Vocational guidance—Juvenile literature. I. Title.
GV1597.V36 2015
793.3023—dc23
                                                                        2014015767

ISBN 978-1-58270-451-7 (hc)
ISBN 978-1-58270-450-0 (pbk)
ISBN 978-1-4442-9929-4 (eBook)

CONTENTS

To Gower
before
what I di
before I ha
of my

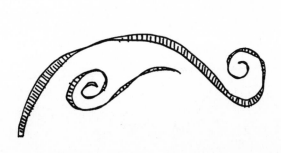

1

Dance Like the World Is Watching: A History of Dance

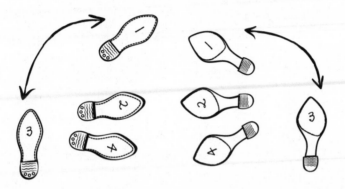

Do you remember the moment when you first thought you wanted to dance? Maybe a friend suggested the idea, or maybe your mom or dad took you to a class to see if you might be interested. Now, do you remember the moment when you realized you *must* dance? That was the truly pivotal moment, the one when you discovered who *you* really are. It is easy enough to want something but much harder to turn that desire into a reality. Only those who *must have* something will succeed at achieving it. You will overcome all obstacles and beat the odds to get what you want.

And if you want to be a dancer, you will face challenges. It takes a tremendous amount of discipline to become a dancer. It is a career that demands the utmost in commitment; this is not an easy life. But if you *must have* it, then you will meet those challenges head-on and you will be fulfilling your passion.

And that is a wonderful life.

QUIZ

Break a Leg! A Dance Career Quiz

1. In my spare time I like to
   A. Swim or do yoga
   B. Watch movie musicals
   C. Go to the mall
   D. Make snacks for my friends or help my parents make dinner
   E. Read dancer biographies

2. At school, I am known as
   A. The athlete
   B. The one with the organized calendar and binders
   C. The one who talks all the time
   D. The one who likes to help when someone gets injured in gym or has a cold
   E. The one who is the first to finish an assignment

3. My idea of a great birthday present is
   A. A new leotard or jazz pants perfect for dancing
   B. Tickets to a Broadway musical
   C. A new video game
   D. A cookbook
   E. A new book about dance

4. My favorite television shows are
   A. Any of the dance competitions like *So You Think You Can Dance*
   B. *Glee*
   C. *Once Upon a Time* or *Face Off*—anything with great costumes and makeup
   D. *Iron Chef*, *Master Chef*, or *Chopped*
   E. Sports analysis shows

5. I am happiest when
    A. I am in the dance studio
    B. I am watching a great television show
    C. I am shopping for new clothes
    D. I am helping my parents in the vegetable garden
       or tending to our windowsill herbs
    E. I am reading

6. I like to read
    A. Sports magazines
    B. Anything I can find about dance and dancers
    C. Scripts
    D. Food blogs
    E. Nonfiction books

7. My favorite movies are
    A. *Happy Feet*
    B. *Footloose*
    C. *Monsters, Inc.*
    D. *Ratatouille*
    E. *Mona Lisa Smile*

8. My favorite place to be is
    A. Performing in the school musical
    B. In the art studio
    C. Working behind the scenes on a
       school play
    D. Eating at a great restaurant
    E. At a bookstore

9. My favorite class in school is
    A. Gym
    B. Choir
    C. English
    D. Science
    E. Social studies

10. I like to listen to
   A. Anything that gets my feet moving
   B. Broadway show albums
   C. Music from famous ballets
   D. Online kids-radio cooking shows
   E. Podcasts about arts and culture

If your answers are mostly *A*s, *B*s, and *C*s, then you may be interested in a career onstage or behind the scenes, as a dancer, artistic director, or marketer.

If you answered mostly *D*s, you may be interested in being a part of a dancer's team, as a chiropractor or a nutritionist.

If you answered mostly *E*s, you may be interested in being an art critic or in photographing dancers.

To Dance Is to Be Human

What is this compulsion we have to move? Are we trying to match our feet, our fingers, our lungs to our heartbeat? Are we trying to connect with the rhythms of the earth? What is this need, this hunger, this passion . . . to dance? The cave paintings and other records of ancient civilizations show dance at the center of human culture. Early people did not consider dance as entertainment but as an essential form of expression. The ancient Egyptians and Greeks incorporated dance into their religious rituals. The Greeks deified dance by honoring Terpsichore, their muse of dance, praying to her for inspiration so that their dances would please and bring them closer to the gods. India and Japan shared this philosophy, and we see their influence centuries later in the works of the founders of modern dance.

The Complex Steps of Asian Dance

Classic Indian dance is made up of three parts: *natya*, which is the drama of the dance; *nritta*, which is the rhythm; and *nritya*, which is the communication of the dance. At first, Hindu dance was taught by gurus or holy men charged with passing on the dances to their students, who would, in turn, pass them on to their students. But given the size of India, there were certain "regionalisms" that crept into the sacred dances. In the southern part of India, the temple dancers were female, their lives dedicated to the service of the gods, so their dancing was soft and alluring. In contrast, the dances in the southwest were hard, and the dancers appeared to be going into battle. The north showed off elegance while the northeast style was delicate and refined. A dancer portraying Shiva, the main god of the Hindu religion, was often cast as the Lord of the Dance, dancing the world into creation.

BY THE NUMBERS: INDIAN DANCE

The movements used in Indian dance are very specific—and numerous. Above the neck, there are:

★ Thirteen positions of the head
★ Thirty-six glances
★ Seven movements of the eyes
★ Nine flutters of the eyelids
★ Seven quirks of the eyebrows
★ Six twitches of the nose
★ Seven shifts of the chin

The neck has nine movements, and there are twenty-four hand gestures, in addition to separate movements for legs and feet. All of these must be coordinated with the music into an intentional dance. Far more complicated than patting your head and rubbing your stomach or walking and chewing gum at the same time!

The dances of Thailand incorporate many of the elements of Indian dance but in ways unique to the Thai people. Before a dancer can perform the traditional dances, he or she must pass two tests. The first requires mastery of a combination of nineteen basic movements. The second requires the dancer to demonstrate balance and composure in the body by dancing to both fast and slow tempos. After passing these tests, the dancers are then qualified to dance solos in one of two different types of theater.

Thai men are accompanied by a male singer who narrates the story while an orchestra supports both the dancers and the storyteller. The costumes are elaborate, made of breathtaking gold-and-silver cloth and with traditional spire headpieces; and this style of Thai dancing is only performed at the royal court.

Thai women perform the *lakon*. The stories for this type of dance came from Thai legends as well as more formal histories. Like the female temple dancers of India, these dancers move in ways that are very feminine, slow, delicate, and refined. And the costumes are stunning, with plumed fans and beautiful fabrics used as props, and set pieces to tell the story.

INSPIRATION FROM ACROSS THE OCEAN

Choreographer Jerome Robbins took his inspiration from *lakon*, a dance Thai women traditionally danced, to create "The Small House of Uncle Thomas" ballet for the second act of the Broadway musical *The King and I*.

Japan is known for *kabuki*, folk dance, and *noh*, religious and ritual dances. Only flute and percussion are used in noh; while in kabuki a group of musicians plays backstage in addition to an onstage use of the *shamisen* (a three-string plucked instrument).

As so many dances around the world have begun, Japanese dance began as rituals of the Shinto religion. Danced by priestesses, noh called upon a divine presence and brought peace to dead souls. The serious noh dramas generally included a bit of light, dialogued theater (think comic relief). These intervals were the beginning of kabuki, the people's art.

Kabuki "officially" became an art form separate from noh when the Shintu priestess, Okumi, danced at a public festival in 1604. This also paved the way for women to perform. Japanese geisha girls, for example, realized their male clients wanted to see kabuki as part of an evening's entertainment. The makeup of kabuki dancers, female and male, is extreme, including faces painted stark white and robes that are heavily decorated.

Comparing these different cultures, it becomes obvious that we have continued to answer our primal needs through dance, driving our bodies forward and demanding more of them in an effort to improve, outdo, and (here is the key word) *revolutionize* what has gone before. It is through a series of such innovations that dance has evolved from tribal storytelling and religious ritual to a structured and systematic art of movement—while remaining a powerful communication tool. And in the Western world, it all began with a wedding.

From France to Italy . . .

During the Middle Ages there were only two dances performed in the European courts. One was a kind of chain dance for which the dancers held hands and "snaked" around in a line. The music was strictly in the background; there was no attempt on the part of the dancers to match their movements to it. The other dance was a very sedate dance—partners held each other by their little fingers as they walked and posed. Though there was some effort to coordinate movement and music, there was not much footwork, and it was not very exciting. Dance was in the doldrums.

Then the cultural shake-up of the Renaissance swept away the cobwebs of old manners and thinking. Art, science, and culture were reborn. In 1533 fourteen-year-old Catherine de Medici of Florence, Italy, married French King Henry II. Fireworks, magicians, and twenty-course meals with peacocks parading across the dining tables were common attractions at this time in Italy, so something even more special was needed for such a royal wedding. An elegant dance called *balletti* was performed in honor of the couple. This dance quickly took hold in France, and newly crowned Queen Catherine used it as publicity for the French court. The French reconstituted the word *balletti* as *ballet*, and dance was on its way to becoming a modern art form.

Center Stage
profile

Name: Alex Castillo
Job: Soloist, Los Angeles Ballet

When did you start dancing and why?
When I was seven or eight. My mom had danced, not professionally; she was more of a tap dancer. She took my brother and me with her to class because there was no babysitter. Sitting in the back watching the class, something came over me and I thought I should try it. The first school I went to was more of a competition studio—it was more tap and jazz with "bootleg ballet." At thirteen, I transferred to Ballet Academy East in New York City. It became my second home. I owe them everything.

Even so dance was merely an interlude during other theatrical works—these performances were rather like today's football half-time shows: just a diversion while people waited for the main show to resume. But a generation later, when Catherine's son, Charles IX, founded the Académie de Poésie et de Musique in 1570, dance became popular. In 1581 the queen's sister, Mademoiselle de Vaudemont, and the king's brother, the Duc de Joyeuse, commissioned the production of *Le Ballet Comique de la Reine* to celebrate their wedding. The lavish drama involved singing and acting as well as dancing (think of it as a sixteenth-century Broadway musical), with the entire production lasting ten and a half hours. The choreography followed many precise geometric patterns, which amazed and delighted the French court.

As Europe moved into the seventeenth century, dance became more and more essential to the French court. King Louis XIII, an excellent dancer himself, starred in many court productions. He also wrote the stories for the ballets and designed costumes. His son, Louis XIV, followed quite literally in his father's footsteps. At age fifteen he danced the central role of the Sun in *Le Ballet de la Nuit* (*The Ballet of the Night*). The thirteen-hour production lived up to its name in that it lasted all night, ending with the dawn and the arrival of the sun, literally and figuratively. Thereafter, Louis XIV was known as *Le Roi de Soleil*, "the Sun King."

Louis XIV is considered the founding father of classical dance. He founded L'Académie de la Danse in 1661, and it was under his influence that the five basic positions of dance were established. As dance was still the province of the nobility (they were the ones footing the bills for these lavish productions, after all), ballets were performed at court, where there was no elevated stage. Costumes were elegant, and dancers wore the fashions of the day. Their shoes were shoes they'd wear in everyday life, made of velvet or leather. As a rule, women were not allowed to perform; Catherine de Medici was the exception. (When you're the queen, you can do as you like.)

While the French were perfecting court ballet, across the Alps in Florence, Italy, the Italians had found a new way to celebrate a royal wedding. In 1589 the guests at the marriage of Ferdinando de Medici, duke of Tuscany, to Queen Catherine's granddaughter, Christine of Lorraine, were entertained by the first opera, *La Pelligrina*. This lengthy production of seven interludes marked the first time that the dancing actually supported the dramatic

9

action rather than functioning just as side entertainment. Given the success of this new musical genre—and not to be outdone by the Italians—the French grabbed the lead again and founded the Paris Opera in 1669. The opera company was housed in a building constructed specially for it. Just over two centuries later, that building became the setting for Gaston Le Roux's serialized novel, *The Phantom of the Opera*. For the first time in modern Western history, the focus shifted away from performances at court, where only members of the nobility could participate, toward a new kind of performer—the professional dancer. A longstanding style and tradition was overturned. The changes were radical. The Sun King, founding father of ballet, now forbade members of his court to perform in any of the operas. If anyone did, that person would lose his noble title. And now, for the first time, women were permitted to assume their rightful place in these performances. The third major change was the introduction of a raised stage complete with a curtain and a proscenium arch frame.

With the building of the Paris Opera House, dance now had an actual theater in which to perform and was finally considered as an art form. The opera house enabled dance to make full use of the theatrical technology of the day, such as trap doors and the special mechanics that allowed dancers to descend from and ascend to the rafters when playing the roles of gods.

As dance technique became more complex, a school for formal training was founded in 1713. The number of professional dancers employed by the Paris Opera expanded from twenty-four to ninety. With the death of Louis XIV in 1715, the first chapter in the history of formal dance closed.

Coffee Really Does Work Wonders

If your parents claim they can't start their day without their morning coffee, neither you nor they may realize that coffee not only changes their day but there was a time when it also changed the world. Due to putrid water conditions, Europeans of the Middle

Ages had to distill their water before it was safe to drink. As a result, they had been liberally downing ale from morning till night, so they were always somewhat off kilter and their days were less productive. With the arrival of a curious bean from Arabia, however, Europe quite literally woke up and smelled the coffee. Coffee houses sprang up all over and became spaces in which people gathered to discuss changes in society and government as well as science and art. The free thinking of the Enlightenment created a revolution in the American Colonies and then in France, and also had an immediate impact upon art in general and dance in particular.

In the 1720s two women, Marie Anne de Cupis de Camargo and Marie Sallé, rivaled each other for supremacy in the Western dance world. Dancing was still "formal," with women corseted and forced to wear hoop skirts that must have felt like the equivalent of wearing a small circus tent. They also had to wear masks. La Camargo had no interest in obeying the conventions of the day, not only as to what women had to wear but also the actual steps they were expected to perform. The Spanish dancer challenged the status quo by executing the demanding jumps, beats, and *tours en l'air* reserved for the male *danseur*. La Camargo cut her skirts shockingly short, to midcalf, to show her exceptional footwork and technique.

Sallé took matters one step further. She didn't just shorten her skirt, she did away with the restrictive wardrobe altogether. According to one observer, Sallé danced the title role in *Pygmallion* "draped in chiffon in the manner of a Greek statue."[1] The simple Greek garb gracefully illustrated the lines of her body, and that was its own revolution. Eventually, her continued disagreements with the Paris Opera prompted Sallé to take her art to London, where she felt she could express herself freely.

Although they were rivals, these two women's efforts completely overturned another century's worth of dance traditions. The focus onstage now shifted away from the danseur and rested squarely on the *danseuse*, ushering in the Romantic Era, which the Italian ballerina Marie Taglioni will forever define. Gone were the stiff shoes of the female dancers punctuating their steps by drumming their heels into the floor. Soft satin slippers replaced the hard, noisy shoes to achieve a silent presentation. The transition to pointe shoes was not far behind.

THE FIVE BASIC POSITIONS

Can you master these positions?

First Position: Legs turned out at the hip, feet angled out, and heels touching. Body standing elegantly erect. This is the "resting" position.

Second Position: Legs turned out from the hip, feet positioned under the shoulders, the backs of the heels facing each other but not touching. This position was designed to accommodate horizontal movement.

Third Position: Legs turned out from the hip and pulled together, the heel of the front foot placed at the instep of the back foot, knees flush together. This position is intended to facilitate forward and backward movement.

Fourth Position: The feet separated by the length of one foot, one foot positioned directly ahead of the other. Legs turned out from the hip, the body balanced in between them. This position is used to transition or pass through from one step or combination to another. It is also used to prepare for and complete pirouettes in *posé*, *arabesque*, and *attitude derriere* and *devant*.

Fifth Position: Similar to third position but with a tighter "fit." Legs turned out from the hip, the heel of the front foot placed in front of the toe of the other. This position allows the dancer to move freely in all directions—forward, backward, and horizontally.

The next ten years produced two defining ballets: *La Sylphide* premiering in Paris in 1832 and *Giselle* in 1841. *Sylphide* was so successful in Europe that Taglioni traveled to Russia to perform it countless times. The country would later have a major impact upon the world dance stage.

Name: Monica Payne
Age: 16
Job (when not studying!): Ballet student
Dream Job: Dancer, American Ballet Theatre

When did you start dancing and why?
I started dancing when I was three. My mom took me to see *The Nutcracker*. I remember watching the Sugar Plum Fairy and seeing how happy she was, and knew I wanted to do that someday. Since then I have loved to dance.

Why did you decide to audition for the School of American Ballet Summer Intensive?
For the experience. It's inspiring. I danced [as] Bluebird from *The Sleeping Beauty*. It really helped me with my turns.

How do you feel about being required to take a class in the contemporary style of dance as part of your ballet training?
The modern helps the ballet; it gets us to move differently. I like to mix it up.

How do you fit school into all of this?
I think we spend too much time in school. The teacher will give us an assignment and I finish the assignment; and I have

to sit there for half an hour and wait for the rest of the class. That's time I could be dancing.

What will you do after high school?
In a perfect world, I would like to be at ABT. But education is important.

What about your social life? What do your friends think about your dancing?
Some of my friends are cheerleaders; and when I tell them I have to go to class or rehearsal, they say, "Can't you skip it?" They don't understand that I have to be here. For them, cheerleading is an activity; for me, dancing is my passion.

● ●

To Russia, with Love

Taglioni's turn in Russia was the product of that country's effort to "catch up" with European thought, art, and culture. When Emperor Peter the Great took the Russian throne in 1689, he was determined to Westernize his country into its own renaissance. French became the language of the Russian court along with French culture, fashion, and art—which included dance. However, there was no "show" in Russian dance, nothing like the Paris Opera. Rather, dance was considered more a manner of behavior or courtly etiquette. (Sounds like the early stages of dance in France, doesn't it?) It really amounted to no more than artificial posturing on the part of the Russian courtiers who were, for the most part, less than thrilled at the tsar forcing European culture upon them.

Peter the Great's daughter, Elizabeth, took the throne in 1741. The new empress loved dancing above all the arts and was an excellent dancer. Her instructor, the French ballet master Jean-Baptiste Landé chose twenty boys and girls, all children of palace servants, to be trained as dancers. Elizabeth increased Landé's responsibilities as *maitre de ballet*, and the dance school held in the upper rooms of the Winter Palace became the foundation for the Imperial Ballet School. But it was an "ordinary" French dancer Marius Petipa whose work stirred the pot again and whose choreography is the touchstone for every ballet dancer today.

Petipa arrived in Russia in 1847, not as a European superstar but as a simple twenty-nine-year-old dancer. Yet he rose from the *corps de ballet* to become ballet master of the Imperial Russian Ballet. As *maitre de ballet*, he took what was and turned it into what is. He married French foundation to Italian athleticism to create the distinct Russian style seen in the now-legendary ballets *The Sleeping Beauty*, *Swan Lake*, and *The Nutcracker*.

SPOTLIGHT

David Hallberg:
A "Big"—Time Honor

David Hallberg has the distinction of being the first American dancer to be invited to perform with Russia's Bolshoi Ballet. The Bolshoi (the name means "big") is older than the United States of America; and Hallberg is not only the first American to dance with the company, he is the first non-Russian to do so.

Hallberg was born in South Dakota but grew up in Arizona. His first introduction to dance was the films of Fred Astaire. He taped nickels to the bottom of his shoes and "tap danced" up and down the neighborhood street. His parents bought him his first pair of real tap shoes when he was nine. He brought them to school for show-and-tell when the other boys brought hockey sticks. This set him up for bullying. "I was the only boy in my environment who danced. It made [me] a target. It was very hurtful."[2]

Fortunately, the Arizona School for the Arts opened, and Hallberg transferred to it. "I found an environment I fit into."[3] He was now able to focus on dance. Under the guidance of the school's dance teacher, Kee-Juan Han, his training blossomed. Han was a tough teacher, but the work paid off. At seventeen, Hallberg was accepted to the Paris Opera Ballet School, and he spent one year in France. He was then asked to join ABT's junior company. After his apprenticeship, he spent three years in the corps before being promoted to soloist. After one year as soloist, he was given the roles and title of principal dancer. While Hallberg was on tour in Russia in 2010, the artistic director of the Bolshoi, Sergei Fillin, saw him dance and offered him the position of *premier danseur* at the Bolshoi. Hallberg struggled with the decision as to whether he should accept the invitations, but in the end he was able to make arrangements to split his time between both companies.

In Russia, ballet is as popular as major sports in America, like football or baseball. Hallberg's first performance as Prince Desiree in *The Sleeping Beauty* was broadcast live to the Russian nation, like the Super Bowl or the World Series are in the United States. Show-and-tell there may be very different than what Hallberg experienced in the States.

From France to Italy . . . to Russia and Back Again

By the turn of the twentieth century, Russian arts supporter Sergei Diaghilev had successfully introduced Russian opera and painting to Western Europe. As the founder of the Ballets Russes dance company, he sent Russian ballet out into the world first via Paris. European dance had now come full circle. The Ballets Russes turned the tables on European ballet. *The Firebird* was based on a

Russian fairy tale. The storyline did not feature a damsel in distress but a brilliant bird. The costumes and sets were exotic; the music by Igor Stravinsky was anything but traditional. The Ballets Russes had the Parisians both on their feet and at its feet at the close of the first season.

By 1917, Imperial Russia was no more. The door to the West bolted shut, and the new communist regime put Russia's art under lock and key for the next seventy-seven years. In the midst of all this upheaval, however, a thirteen-year-old student of what had been the Imperial Ballet School quietly began plotting his own revolution. Increasingly frustrated by the repression of the communist government, Georgi Balanchivadze first escaped Russia for Western Europe in 1920 and then headed on to the United States, where he would become known as George Balanchine, the man who would reinvent classical dance in ways that no one could have ever imagined.

By 1917, Imperial Russia was no more. The door to the West bolted shut, and the new communist regime put Russia's art under lock and key for the next seventy-seven years. In the midst of all this upheaval, a thirteen-year-old student of what was the Imperial Ballet School quietly began plotting his own revolution. Increasingly frustrated by the repression of the communist government, Georgi Balanchivadze first escaped Russia for Western Europe in 1920 and then headed on to the United States, where he would become known as George Balanchine, the man who would reinvent classical dance in ways that no one could have ever imagined.

AVOIDING THE PITFALLS OF BODY IMAGE

Dancers are athletes, so there is no avoiding the importance of the body—or that a dancer's body needs to be fit. There's also no denying that each ballet company will encourage a certain look among its dancers; so if you're interested in joining that company, you should study its company's style and body type.

Some types are very specific, and even the best dancer in the world, if he or she does not look like that type, will not be chosen. The Balanchine ballerina has a certain look: a few inches taller than the average dancer (five feet seven and up), with a short torso and longer-than-average legs. When you audition for NYCB, you are measured thoroughly, right down to the extension of your foot. While most ballet dancers are thin due to the energy used during practice and performance, Balanchine took thinness several steps further in order to achieve uniformity in the look of his ballets. (Watch his production of *Serenade* and you'll get the idea.) Balanchine was quoted as stating, "Ballet is woman,"[4] and he was very particular as to how he wanted his female dancers to look.

Robert Joffrey, on the other hand, welcomed diversity in his dancers. There is no uniform body type for a Joffrey dancer. Principal dancer April Daly explained, "The Joffrey, because it is so diverse and we do so many different works, you almost need to have different kinds of dancers to do the different ballets. So, there is the tall, there's the shorter, there's the more athletic."[5]

Height, size, race—Joffrey celebrated the uniqueness of his dancers and knew how to blend them into a cohesive whole without sacrificing their individuality. This was revolutionary.

Eating disorders are a serious issue in dance, especially when a certain look seems to be expected. It is a danger that as the physical demands upon the dancer increase, so does the pressure to be thinner. You want to be careful that you don't let that look overrun your life.

The average person uses up 1,200 calories a day; the average dancer burns up 1,700-2,000 per day.[6] You have to replace those spent calories with consumed calories—food!—in order to keep your body in balance and stay healthy. If you do develop an eating disorder, you don't just lose weight; your body's metabolism gets out of whack, resulting in hormonal imbalances, destabilized systems, and other internal complications in your organs. The average age for the onset of an eating disorder is between nine and twelve. If you think you might be tipping toward an eating disorder or fear you are already caught in that downward-spiraling vortex, talk to your family, your dance teacher, or another trusted adult. You will likely want to seek professional help immediately.

Dance's focus on the body does not have to be negative. Through dance, we celebrate the amazing human form and all that it can do. Dancers strive for the best fitness, which is a healthy goal to have. Sixteen-year-old Monica Payne, a ballet dancer who is featured in a youth profile earlier in this chapter, said, "I focus on eating healthy. We need to give our bodies the right energy. If I'm getting ready for a performance, I try to eat more fruit and vegetables. I ask my mom not to buy junk food." That's the right attitude!

2

Rise Up: Ballet as the Foundation of Dance

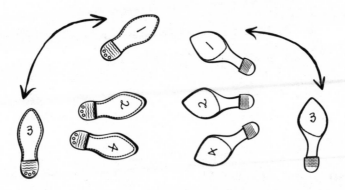

Ballet is the foundation of all dance. The French terminology is used in every dance discipline. It is from this foundation that you will become flexible and able to learn any choreographic style. So, no matter what avenue of dance you want to pursue, your career as a dancer begins at the barre.

Educate Your Body

The training for a dancer starts early. Most will start dance class at age four or five, but professional training starts age eight or ten. It may seem overwhelming to have to make a career decision this early in life, but anyone who wants to become an athlete (and dancers are athletes) simply must do this.

A Day in the Life of a Ballet Student

From New York to Los Angeles, Paris to London, Rome to St. Petersburg, it's pretty much the same: practice happens every day.

First Class: Technique Class
A half-hour at the barre; a half-hour in the center; the last half-hour *en pointe* for girls, while boys work on beats and big jumps.

Second Class: Pointe and Variation (for Girls) or Men's Class (for Boys)
In this class, students practice the solos from such ballets as *The Sleeping Beauty*, *Swan Lake*, and *Giselle*.

Third Class: *Pas de Deux*
Everyone comes together to learn partnering, including supported turns and lifts.

Fourth Class: Rehearsal
For the final component of the day, the students practice for whatever production is coming up.

Name: Anatalia Hordov
Age: 14
Job (when not studying!): Ballet student
Dream Job: Dancer, San Francisco Ballet

When did you start dancing and why?
When I was three. I was following in my sister's footsteps. I was always dancing around the house so my mom put me in dance class so I would have the proper space.

Why did you decide to audition for the Youth America Grand Prix in New York, the largest ballet competition in the world?

For the experience. I danced Swanilda's variation from Act III of *Coppélia*. It was very exciting. There was one evening where we got to dance at Lincoln Center.

How do you feel about being required to take a class in contemporary style of dance as part of your ballet training?

I actually love contemporary. I think it's really important to have it, especially since so many of the big ballet companies are doing contemporary work now.

How do you fit school into all of this?

I'm good at time management. I find any time I can to do homework. I go to the library during lunch and use free periods so that when I go to dance class after school, I can just concentrate on dancing.

What will you do after high school?

I want to see where my dancing takes me. Why can't I go far? I'm thinking about San Francisco Ballet. I saw some of their principal dancers at the gala at the Youth America Grand Prix.

What about your social life? What do your friends think about your dancing?

A lot of my friends are in arts programs at school (like music), so they understand my dancing.

●○●○●○●○●○●○●○●○●○●○●○●○●○●○●○●

Whether amateur or professional, you must always be working on your craft. Professional dancers take company class every day and also go to different teachers in their area (New York is full of them) to get "that something different." There is always something new to discover, and that is the fun part. You will never know it all, which is what will keep you going—that hunger to learn, improve and perfect. If you ever think you do know it all, eat a large slice of humble pie and get to the nearest class immediately.

Six Ballet Techniques—and Lots of Firebrand Dancers

There are six different techniques in ballet: French, Bournonville, Cecchetti, Russian, Balanchine, and Royal Academy of Dance (RAD). Let's talk about each.

French

France is the founding nation of ballet. It is the home of the Paris Opera, the oldest ballet company in the world and forever immortalized by the artist Edgar Degas with his paintings and sculptures of the ballet apprentices of the Opera. Paris was considered *the* center of culture and art at the beginning of the twentieth century, which is why Diaghilev premiered his Ballets Russes there. The Paris Opera began hiring Russian dancers, including the two prominent Imperial Russian ballerinas Mathilde Kschessinska and Olga Preobrazhenskaya. Refugees from the Russian Revolution, they moved to Paris and opened studios there.

Bournonville

The Bournonville technique originated in Denmark and is known for its speed and technical difficulty. However, the Bournonville style demands that the work *not* be presented in a flamboyant manner. There are no huge jumps, no extreme extensions. The son of a French dancer, August Bournonville was known for his incredibly fast footwork and multiple *pirouettes*—seven turns from one preparation. For the dancer, there is also no margin of error in Bournonville choreography; the smallest error in the difficult *enchainment* is immediately apparent.

Cecchetti

The Cecchetti technique is named after Italian ballet master Enrico Cecchetti. Short and stocky, he was an exciting dancer with many bold and brash moves, and a knack for staging ballets. When he danced in Russia in 1887, he was invited to take positions as principal dancer and second ballet master at the tsar's Imperial Theaters. It is from Cecchetti that the Russians acquired the spectacular thirty-two *fouettés*, exceptionally long balances and extraordinary leaps and beats, which they then refined so they could be seamlessly incorporated into the existing Russian technique.

Name: Allynne Noelle
Job: Principal ballerina, Los Angeles Ballet

When did you start dancing and why?
When I was five. My best friend asked me to come with her to ballet class, and that was it. By eight or nine, I knew I wanted to dance professionally. By the time I was thirteen, my mom jumped on board and asked my teacher if she thought I had what it takes. I studied Cecchetti technique. It was very strict, unaffected, clean, and classical. We had exams up to age fifteen.

Russian

The Fundamentals of Dance, by the Russian ballerina Agrippina Vaganova, set the Russian technique to paper. Published in 1933, the manual united the Italian flair for jumps and turns with the original French foundation, liberally peppered with what was distinctly Russian.

Balanchine

George Balanchine, the twentieth-century rebel of the Russian Ballet, deplored the labored transitions and long preparations of the Imperial Ballet technique. When he came to the United States in 1934, he founded the School of American Ballet (SAB) to train dancers in his "revised" version of the Russian ballet. Everything in Balanchine is bigger, higher, faster. This is the style of the New York City Ballet.

Royal Academy of Dance (RAD)

A combination of the best French, Italian (Cecchetti), Danish (Bournonville), and Russian (Vaganova) techniques blended together into a cohesive whole, the Royal Academy of Dance method was developed in Great Britain. RAD has structured levels with a specific syllabus for each level. A student must master the requirements of the syllabus then pass an exam before moving up in the levels.

Pointe at This

So, you have now faithfully taken class for several years, studied and practiced your technique, and achieved strength and flexibility. For the ladies, it's time to answer that ever-burning question: when can I go on pointe?

But first, why go on pointe at all?

ANATOMY OF A POINTE SHOE

Although there are many different makers and styles of the pointe shoe, the basic anatomy is a constant.

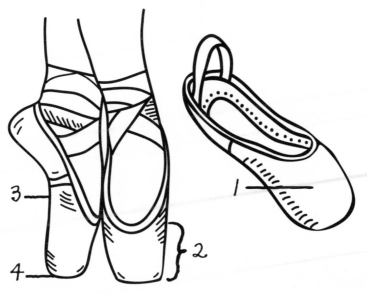

1. The **box** is the hard part of the shoe constructed of layers of satin and glue.

2. The **vamp** is the distance between the drawstring knot and the top edge of the box (at your toes). The vamp can be cut high or low depending on the individual dancer's foot.

3. The **shank** is the spine of the shoe. It is a light piece of wood that runs the length of the shoe and is attached under the insole, supporting the foot while the dancer is on full pointe.

4. The **platform** is at the tip of the shoe and is flat. This is the balance point. It can be narrow or wide depending on dancer preference, which is determined by the anatomy of the dancer's feet.

The History of Pointe

Once dance moved to the stage, the audience was looking up at the dancers. As the view was "feet first," the dancers' feet became more important. In an effort to make the ballerina appear lighter and extend the line of her leg, several dancers of the early nineteenth century began experimenting with dancing on the tips of their toes. Marie Taglioni is credited with being the first to really dance *en pointe* in *La Sylphide*. To be sure, other dancers had risen on the tips of their toes prior to Taglioni's historical performance, but they were either assisted by wires or stood on their toes only briefly. Taglioni is the first to really use pointe work as a technique.

There was nothing special about her shoes. Taglioni simply darned the tips of her existing slippers, which were really nothing more than satin street shoes. There was no stiffened box to protect the toes, no wood shank to support the foot. Taglioni danced on pointe through sheer willpower, spurred on by the incentive of not being outdone by other ballerinas who were well on their way to accomplishing this feat themselves. Taglioni put herself through exhausting physical training in order to appear weightless and her dancing effortless.

MEN ON POINTE?

Gentlemen, you will rarely if ever be asked to dance on pointe. That said, Frederick Ashton's choreography for *A Midsummer Night's Dream* does require the character of Bottom to don a pair of pointe shoes for comic effect when he is turned into a donkey, the pointes becoming his "hooves." The only other exceptions that come to mind are those courageous men who work on pointe in *Les Ballets Trocadero de Monte Carlo* and, believe or not, do some moves in hip-hop.

By the late 1800s, the Italians were the reigning virtuosos of pointe work. Ballerina Carlotta Brianza balanced (seemingly) endlessly and effortlessly as Aurora in "The Rose Adagio" in the original production of *The Sleeping Beauty*. Pierina Legnani created her own technical fireworks when she whipped off thirty-two *fouettés* in the third act of *Swan Lake*. Pointe work now brought a certain excitement and brilliance to ballet.

AVOIDING THE PITFALLS OF POINTE WORK

Ballet is a beautiful art form, but nothing about it is natural. When trained correctly, however, you will not be damaging yourself for life. You will be in terrific shape, and the art form will become natural to you as you continue to develop your technique. As part of proper training, take proper care of yourself, from start to finish.

Have feet that are naturally suited for pointe shoes. Just as tall people are, generally speaking, better suited for basketball than are short people, and people with bigger lungs usually are better able to swim than those with smaller lungs, so natural body shape matters in dance. This does not make any one person better or worse than any other; nor does it mean someone who "looks like a dancer" can actually dance better than someone who doesn't. But, everything else being equal (ability, motivation, dedication), foot shape can help.

The ideal foot for pointe work has a high instep, and its first three toes are of equal length. This makes it much easier to balance, as you can extend and use all three toes. The less-than-ideal foot has a low arch and/or the second toe is longer than the big toe. This construction causes the second toe to "knuckle under" so that when you rise on pointe, you end up balancing on approximately one square inch of your big toe. But do not despair; it can be done. You will just have to work harder from your center to pull up off your feet. What an incredibly strong dancer you will become as a result!

First and foremost: get fitted correctly for shoes. Go to a professional fitter (your teacher will be able to recommend someone) and ask your teacher to either accompany you or inspect your shoes when you bring them to the studio.

There are many different makes of pointe shoes. You will find the brand that best suits you through experimentation. Also, expect your preferences to change over time. When you are first starting pointe work, you will more than likely want a sturdy shoe. As you progress in your training and become stronger on pointe, you will probably start to gravitate toward a lighter shoe.

If you have a high arch, you will most likely want a high vamp to help prevent you from overarching and breaking the shank. If you don't have a high instep, you will want a low vamp so that you can get your foot over your toes. There are also exercises you can do to strengthen your arches. Depending on the shape of your foot and the configuration of your toes, you may want a narrower or broader platform.

Break in your pointe shoes. Breaking in a pair of pointe shoes is rarely anyone's idea of a good time. The shank will feel stiff and unwilling to bend while the box, which is made to be hard, prevents you from "feeling the floor" when balancing on full pointe or on the flat. The stiff box is also loud, which ruins the aesthetic of being light on your feet when you are heard clomping all over the stage. Despite some of the advancements made in the manufacturing of pointe shoes, there is not a ballerina on the planet who is not very particular about the brand of shoe she wears and how they fit. This is why professional ballerinas always have several pairs of "broken in" pointe shoes on hand in their dressing rooms so they can exchange them over the course of a performance. Try these tricks of the trade for customizing your pointe shoes:

★   First, pull out the drawstring. It is there strictly for cosmetic effect, and is actually both useless and an annoyance.

★ Next, gently bend the shank back and forth with your hands, arching it then flexing it backward. This will help loosen it up and make it more pliable and receptive, allowing you to "roll through" your feet.

★ Last but not least, to soften the box, you can use the hammer technique and literally smash it with a hammer. You can also try steaming the box over a teakettle. When the water boils and steam comes out of the spout, hold the shoe over the spout so that the steam goes directly up into the box. Let the shoe steam for thirty to forty-five seconds. Remove the shoe from the spout and immediately put it on your foot. Repeat with the second shoe and then wear them around the house until they have completely cooled, usually about thirty minutes. Do *not* rise on pointe while the boxes are still warm. Once they have cooled, take the shoes off and let them continue to "air out" overnight. This reshapes the shoe to your individual foot, making it much more comfortable to dance and easier to balance on pointe.

Of course the not-so-happy truth is that once you have your pointe shoes broken in and comfortable, they only have a couple of hours left before they teeter toward extinction. When the box of your pointe shoes starts to feel too soft, you can safely prolong the life of your shoes with Krazy Glue. Just coat the inside of the box with the glue, and place the shoes on a cookie sheet. Bake them in a low oven (with the temperature set under 200 degrees) for about thirty minutes. Let them cool overnight. This method can help your shoes last for another week. After that, you will want to rip the shanks out and wear your old pointe shoes for the barre and technique class. Recycling your old shoes will improve your balance in center work, as the majority of your performances will be in pointe shoes. It is a far different experience balancing "on the flat" in pointe shoes than it is in simple ballet slippers.

Protect your tootsies: minimize blisters. Your toes will blister—it's an occupational hazard—but you can help them blister less. There are differently weighted gel pads that slip over all your toes, and there are "toe tubes," which look like a glove for your toes. "Toe socks," can be cut to size and placed over each individual toe. You can also wrap each toe with surgical tape, pull on your tights, and put on your pointe shoes without any additional padding or protection. This causes the least interference between how your foot fits in the shoe and how well you can balance on the floor. However you decide to protect your toes, you must always be able to feel the floor when you are up on pointe. Your balance point is much narrower in pointe shoes, and you have to feel the floor underneath you to know where to place your center

Protect your tootsies: prepare for aches and pains. In addition to blisters, you can also expect bruised or ingrown toenails and bunions. Expect to spend a fair amount of time soaking your feet in hot water and epsom salts. (It's a great time to study and do your homework!) For injuries beyond bruising, you should see a podiatrist, preferably one who specializes in dance and sports medicine.

Made in the USA

There are many ballet companies in the United States—large and small, cosmopolitan and regional, world renowned and homegrown. The first ballet companies founded in this country are American Ballet Theatre (ABT) and New York City Ballet (NYCB).

The Big Three (ABT, NYCB, Joffrey) and Others

American Ballet Theatre emerged from the strong will and large bank account of American heiress Lucia Chase. With the help of Russian *émigré* Mikhail Mordkin, a former Bolshoi dancer who fled Russia after the Revolution, Chase formed American Ballet Theatre with the intent of presenting to the American public a wide range of classic ballets from every major artistic period in ballet history. Given that the year was 1939 and World War II was raging across Europe, the fledgling company was able to draw upon the talents of fellow Russian refugees such as Mikhail Fokine and Bronislava Nijinska (sister of the famous Vaslav Nijinsky).

The distinct Russian Imperial influence is still evident today: ABT is best known for its elaborate productions of the "big ballets." While the company has certainly evolved over the decades and welcomed new works by twentieth-century choreographers such as Twyla Tharp's *Push Comes to Shove*, Antony Tudor's *The Leaves Are Fading*, Jerome Robbins's *Dancers at a Gathering*, and some of George Balanchine's work, ABT remains Russian at its roots.

Coming up at the same time in the same city was New York City Ballet. Though George Balanchine trained in the Vagonova technique at the Russian Imperial Ballet School in St. Petersburg, he wanted to take ballet in a new direction. Balanchine was considered the founder of neoclassical ballet, and his most notable works include *Apollo*, *Concerto Barocco*, *Serenade*, *Chaccone*, and his exuberant tribute to America, *Stars and Stripes*. Balanchine wanted his choreography to be presented in its purest form—dance for the sake of dance alone. As a general rule, his ballets have no story, no sets, and the simplest of costumes so that the line of the dancers' bodies is always clean and uncluttered.

Then in 1948, Seattle-born Robert Joffrey arrived in New York with the intention of pursuing a career in ballet. He quickly realized, however, that the Big Apple had only two viable ballet companies, neither of which he considered to be truly American. From the time he was eleven years old, Joffrey wanted to have his own ballet company. "I always felt that it was important that we represent our country and that we have ballets that are created by Americans and on American themes and when possible, using American music,"[1] Joffrey stated. He did all of that and more. Joffrey started his company with six dancers whom he had trained at his school in New York. Traveling the country in a borrowed station wagon, they brought ballet to small towns that had little or no exposure to the art form. They became known as "the Johnny Appleseeds of dance."

Now there are many ballet companies that would live up to Joffrey's expectations: the San Francisco Ballet has an excellent reputation, as do the Pennsylvania Ballet in Philadelphia, Houston Ballet, Miami City Ballet, Boston Ballet, Ballet West in Salt Lake City, Los Angeles Ballet, Washington Ballet, and a host of others.

Ballet Is for All

Ballerinas are frequently thought of as being caucasian. But think again! There is a rich history of dancers, past and present, of different races.

Teenager Michaela DePrince is a superb ballerina in the making. She recently joined the ranks of the Dance Theatre of Harlem. DTH was founded by former NYCB dancer Arthur Mitchell. Mitchell was the first African American to become a member of NYCB, and he danced with the company for fifteen years. He left the company to create "a world of beauty and grace in the slums of Harlem."[2] Misty Copeland, an African American dancer from Southern California, was promoted to soloist at ABT in 2013. A winner of the Spotlight Awards at age fifteen, Copeland was advised to go into contemporary dance because of her skin color, but she wanted to dance in a ballet company. She was in the ABT corps for seven years before her promotion. While her personal goal is to become the first African American principal ballerina with ABT, she has another driving force: "For young African-Americans to feel that they have a chance to see a brown face on the stage, that ballet isn't this white world untouchable to them—I think having that visual does so much. I think it's so important for them to see me and to hear me."[3]

Ballet Hispanico, founded in 1970 by Venezuelan American dancer Tina Ramirez, also strives to remind people that ballet has never been and should never be a whites-only art. Ballet Hispanico converted two carriage houses on West Eighty-Ninth Street in New York City to house its six studios and company of Latin American dancers. Its work joins the dance cultures of Cuba, Trinidad, Puerto Rico, Mexico, Spain, Argentina, Colombia, and, of course, Venezuela with classic and contemporary techniques to create a specifically Latin form of concert dance. The company has now performed for over two million people, touring eleven countries and three continents.

Arthur Mitchell: Driven to Dance

As a kid, Arthur Mitchell was "driven to dance." That would not have been unusual, except that he was a black kid living in the slums of Harlem in New York City in the 1940s. He loved musicals, so he rented a top hat and tails to audition for the High School of Performing Arts, singing and dancing Fred Astaire's famous "Steppin' Out with My Baby" number from the movie *Easter Parade*. "They took me not because I was good but because I had so much nerve,"[4] he said. While his teachers were quick to recognize his talent, they encouraged him to target modern dance companies, as they would be more receptive to the color of his skin. But Mitchell wanted to be a ballet dancer.

He went on to win a scholarship to the School of American Ballet and, at the age of twenty-one, he became a member of the New York City Ballet. He was the first African American to join the company, and Balanchine created roles specifically for him. "Do you know what it took for Balanchine to put me, a black man, onstage with a white woman? This was 1957, before civil rights,"[5] Mitchell stated in an interview with in the *Los Angeles Times*. Balanchine had always wanted a culturally diversified ballet company and addressed any questions of race by stating simply,

35

"If Mitchell doesn't dance, New York City Ballet doesn't dance."[6] Mitchell remained with the company for fifteen years.

But in 1969, after the assassination of Martin Luther King, Jr., Mitchell decided that he had to do even more to further the world of dance. He established a school of classical dance for Harlem's children. No child was turned away. After rehearsing in a converted two-story garage, Dance Theatre of Harlem danced its first performance in 1971 at the Guggenheim Museum in Manhattan. Highly praised by the dance critics, the company made tremendous strides over the next three decades. It staged its own productions of *The Firebird* and *Scheherazade* in addition to a full-length production of *Giselle* with a twist. *Creole Giselle* used all the original choreography from the nineteenth century, but it was set in pre–Civil War Louisiana instead of Germany.

Despite its many successes, Dance Theatre of Harlem suffered financial problems, and the company disbanded in 2004. The school, however, continued; and although it took nine long years to reconstitute, the company was back on its feet as of April 5, 2013.

Go Global

Just as choreographers learn and borrow from dancers across the world, these days no ballet company is exclusive to one country—they are all international.

For example, ABT was quick to welcome Mikhail Baryshnikov and Natalia Makarova when each defected from Russia. The company is consistently populated by people from all over the world. Principal dancer Paloma Herrera is from Argentina, and rising rapidly through the ranks; and Hee Seo, a Korean ballerina, was recently promoted to principal dancer. New York City Ballet is headed by Peter Martins, a Dane, who danced with the company for sixteen years before Balanchine handpicked him to inherit and carry on his legacy.

All this international exchange and influence has certainly improved the state of dance as an art form as members from each company "borrow" steps, phrasing, and techniques from one another. When Russia's Bolshoi Ballet invited ABT principal dancer David Hallberg to join the company as *premier danseur,* Hallberg stated, "[Russians] have a different style of dancing and that's part of the reason I wanted to go . . . to learn their style."[7]

RUSSIAN BALLERINA PLAYS THE VAUDEVILLE CIRCUIT

It is hard to imagine, but ballet entered American culture through the back door of the vaudeville houses. After World War I and the Russian Revolution, Russia's prima ballerina Anna Pavlova toured the thriving network of American vaudeville theaters. Billed as "Pavlova the Incomparable," her beautiful, lyric signature solo, *The Dying Swan,* was sandwiched in-between trained elephants and minstrel shows.

Get There from Here

Find the Right School or Program

Finding the right ballet school is a must. Correct training at the beginning of your dance career can make all the difference. If you and your parents are coming at dance "cold," invest some of your time in learning about your options.

★ Check with your friends who are enrolled at a dance studio and their parents for recommendations.

★ Ask the staff at local dance shops who they would recommend.

★ Use the internet to look up different studios, finding out about their summer intensive programs, learning what their audition process is, determining what the cost is, and noting when and where their auditions are held. You should also be able to find rehearsal and performance footage of these companies on YouTube. Observe the difference in the way a variation or *pas de deux* is danced in rehearsal as compared to how it is danced in performance.

When you find a couple of studios you're interested in, ask them if you can watch a class. (You should always be able to do this.) And if your interest is in ballet, it is best to attend a school that emphasizes training ballet dancers.

From the Classroom to the Stage

As you research various ballet companies to learn about their audition processes, investigate their associated schools as well.

★ The School of American Ballet was founded with the intention that some of the students would become part of New York City Ballet.

★ ABT has the Jacqueline Kennedy Onassis School in New York in addition to having established a relationship with the University of North Carolina School of the Arts.

★ The Joffrey Ballet, Kansas City Ballet, Houston Ballet, and many other companies have relationships with ballet schools.

As a student or apprentice to one of these companies, you work hard while waiting for the invitation to take a company class. This is usually the first step to being considered to join the company.

Find the Right Teacher

It is also very important that you work with someone who can recognize your needs, build your confidence, and inspire you. You must be relaxed in class and given the freedom to learn new steps and try new combinations. You must feel so comfortable in class that if you fall out of turn or land poorly after a jump, you will be able to shrug it off and try again. Ballet is very demanding. Rarely are you going to get anything right on the first attempt. Believe it or not, that's the fun of it—facing the challenges of dance and conquering them. It's exhilarating! But you must have a teacher who is thoroughly invested in you and your success. You *do* want constructive criticism; it's the only way you will improve.

Read

Read publications like *Dance Magazine*, *Pointe*, *Dance Spirit*, and *Dance Teacher*. All have electronic as well as print subscriptions. You should also be able to find them at your local bookstore, newsstand, or library. These publications will keep you in the loop as to what is happening in the dance world. Read the articles and look at the ads for various competitions and conventions. You will find supplements in these magazines with comprehensive listings of these events around the country.

Compete

Competitions are an excellent way to gain experience, and there are quite a few related to ballet: New York International Ballet Competition, USA International Ballet Competition, and the largest in the world, the Youth America Grand Prix.

The Grand Prix was founded by Larissa Saveliev, a former dancer with Russia's famous Bolshoi Ballet. The purpose of the competition is to give young dancers exposure to the "world's elite" in ballet. Company directors from all over the world come to this competition. "So many dancers like to have a career but very, very, very few succeed," said Saveliev in the documentary

First Position. "You have to have the right physique, you have to have technique, you have to have the right financial situation." The competition is held in New York, so if you do not live nearby, you will have to travel there if you are selected as a finalist. This also means staying in a hotel for the week of the actual competition, which is another expense. In addition, you have to include the costs of coaching before you go and during; choreography for your contemporary variation; costuming; and many, many pairs of pointe shoes (if you are female). It can be expensive to compete, but the payoff is dancing for and meeting professional dancers, choreographers, and judges. There are three categories assigned in the Grand Prix: ages nine through eleven, twelve through fourteen, and fifteen through nineteen. As in the Olympics, gold, silver, and bronze medals are awarded in each category. But winning isn't everything; scholarships, apprenticeships, and contracts to major ballet companies worldwide are offered to those who catch the judges' attention.

 SPOTLIGHT

Michaela DePrince: Not Just a Number

Born in conflicted Sierra Leone, Michaela DePrince was orphaned at age four. Her father was killed by rebels, and her mother died one week later from starvation. Her uncle abandoned her at an orphanage where the children were given numbers according to their "adoptability," number one being the most adoptable. Out of twenty-seven children, she was labeled #27, the least desirable. It was in this orphanage where she saw a picture of a ballet dancer on a torn cover of a magazine and was fascinated by it.

Fortunately, Michaela was adopted by a family in Philadelphia, and DePrince began her new life and her dance training when she came to the United States. However, as she stated in the documentary *First Position*, "Everyone knows that black girls can't dance ballet." DePrince proved them wrong when, at age fourteen, she became one of the finalists in the 2011 Youth America Grand Prix, winning a scholarship to ABT's Jacqueline Kennedy Onassis School in New York. Upon graduating from the JKO School, she made her professional debut with the South African Ballet at age seventeen, dancing the lead role of Gulnare in *Le Corsair*. DePrince has since joined the newly reconstituted Dance Theatre of Harlem.

Dress for Success

By looking at photos and video online or maybe even visiting a school, pay attention to what dancers are wearing in class and in rehearsal. When you audition for or take a summer intensive program, you will want to look like you fit in with that company. Sometimes dancers creatively layer leg warmers, sweaters, baggy pants, and sweatpants, but when in doubt, opt for "less is more." You will want a professional appearance so that the judges at your audition can see your line and technique easily. For ballet, you can't go wrong with a black leotard, pink tights, and pointe shoes for the girls; and black leggings and white T-shirts for the guys. Hair needs to be pulled back and secured up and off the face. When you are doing your multiple *pirouettes* and *tours en l'air*, you want those judging you to be watching your technique, not your hair flying around. They might wonder if you can even see where you are going!

ACTIVITY
Get Ready to Pointe

Once you have the proper shoes, you will begin your pointe work at the barre. Do not attempt pointe work on your own; get the okay from your ballet instructor that you—and your shoes—are ready. Then allow your ballet instructor to lead you through specific exercises. But this list will give you an idea of what to expect.

1. With both hands on the barre, stand in first position and roll up through your feet onto full pointe and back down.

2. Stand in a modified second position, again roll up to full point, *plié* while pushing out the instep, straighten both legs, and roll down.

3. Stand in second position with both hands on the barre and bend the right leg, placing the right foot on full pointe. Put your weight over your right toes and push the instep out. Repeat on the left foot. This exercise is called "pushovers," and it helps strengthen the instep for pointe work.

4. Place a book one inch thick on the floor. In bare feet, place the toes of one foot over the spine of the book. Roll up through the foot to *demi pointe*, spreading your toes as flat as possible over the spine as you work toward full *élevé*. Roll back down through the foot. Repeat the exercise eight times and then switch feet to strengthen weak arches.

3

Broadway and Hollywood, or Hollywood and Broadway?

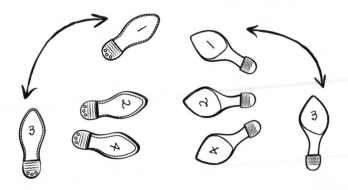

In 2007, *Dancing with the Stars* made its American debut on television and the interest in dance in the United States exploded. Suddenly, it seemed dance was everywhere. Another dance competition, *So You Think You Can Dance*, popped up. *Bunheads*, based on the book of the same name, became a popular series on the ABC Family Channel. Though it only lasted two seasons, *Smash* went behind the scenes of the Broadway musical. There has been a remake of the movie *Footloose*, the movie *Step Up* has had two sequels, and dancers are being used more and more in commercials.

Would you like to be one of those kids dancing on a Broadway stage? Do you get chills when you hear the sound of a Broadway pit orchestra? Do you enjoy the adrenalin kick of performing on a stage in front of a live audience? Are you thrilled by the electric charge of applause at the end of a number? Then prepare yourself: if you want to trod the boards of Broadway, you have to be a triple threat.

GREAT YOUNG PEOPLE ON THE GREAT WHITE WAY

At no time in Broadway history had there been so many kids working on the Great White Way (coined when the street was first illuminated by electric lights) as in the 2011-2012 season. The musicals using young talent were:

A Christmas Story (based on the movie)

Motown, the Musical

The revival of *Annie*

The British import *Matilda, the Musical* (based on the book)

Bring It On

Newsies (based on the movie)

It was difficult to find a Broadway musical that season that *wasn't* using kids, all of them dancing up a storm!

A triple threat is a dancer who sings and acts, or a singer who dances and acts, or an actor who dances and sings. The first definition is really the most accurate—the dancer who sings and acts. Do you really have to do all three to work in a Broadway musical? Yes. Absolutely. No question.

Center Stage *profile*

Name: Jeff Rizzo
Job: Music conductor

When did you start this job and why?

At first I thought I wanted to be an actor. I was thirteen when I did my first musical, *Oliver* at Sacramento Music Theatre in California. I didn't know there was such a job as a music conductor, but over the course of doing the show, I realized that there was a guy in charge of the music. Since music was "my thing," I thought I could have a career as a musical director rather than acting. My first show as conductor was *You're a Good Man, Charlie Brown* in Sacramento.

When did dancers become singers too?

The shift happened with *A Chorus Line*. It used to be that dancers sang in "the key of low," but now it's rare to find a dancer who can't cut it. It's always great when a dancer sings well. We've come to expect it.

What does a Broadway musical conductor look for in a dancer's voice?

A strong voice. They don't have to have a great voice, but they [do] have to hold pitch and learn parts and hold the harmonies. All the dancers have to sing. Sometimes they are hired for a look, but that doesn't mean I don't expect them to do what they need to do. They don't hire as many for the chorus now, so everybody does it all.

What is the best way to get singing experience?

Sing in school choirs, church choirs, school musicals. Anything where you have to hold pitch and harmonies. Of course, singing lessons are good.

While the musical director of a Broadway show is not usually looking for operatic voices, it is obvious you will need to have some experience singing if you want to work on Broadway. But it wasn't always that way.

A Series of Evolutions and Revolutions

A combination of melodrama, British light opera (like the works of Gilbert and Sullivan), and good old American vaudeville, the underpinnings of American musical theater date back to just after the American Revolutionary War. *The Temple of Minerva* was a short work of two scenes performed in 1781 as part of a concert given by the French minister in honor of George Washington. First staged in Philadelphia, it was designed to sing the praises of the alliance between France and the newly formed United States of America. Short as it was, *Minerva* featured the first music written by an American for the American stage. Its expensive, fancy sets also laid the foundations for two pivotal productions that followed a century later: *The Black Crook* and *Ziegfeld Follies*.

As is the case with so many important events, the production of *The Black Crook* was a happy accident. In 1866, as the country was recovering from the Civil War, two theatrical producers, Henry C. Jarrett and Harry Palmer, booked a French ballet company to dance at the Academy of Music in New York City. Then that theater burned to the ground. Desperate to find a theater for the soon-to-arrive dancers, the two men appealed to the manager of another theater, William Wheatley, but he had already scheduled a melodrama. Jarrett and Palmer convinced Wheatley to combine the two traveling troupes into one production. The result was *The Black Crook*, a five-and-a-half-hour spectacular that dazzled New York audiences and ran for an unheard of (at that time) 475 performances.

The critic for the *New York Times* exclaimed, "The ballet, the wonderful ballet . . . was the thing."[1] The choreography was in the Romantic style of the day (like Taglioni's *La Sylphide*) and featured four ballerinas: Ria Sangalli, Rose Delval, Betty Rigl, and Marie Bonafanti (the same Marie Bonafanti who later taught Ruth St. Denis and Isadora Duncan). The set changes were done as transformations in full view of the audience. The special effects were unlike anything seen before. The reviewer for the *New York Tribune* raved: "One by one, curtains of mist ascend and drift away. Silver couches on which the fairies loll . . . ascend and descend amid a silver rain. Columns of living splendor whirl, and dazzle as they whirl. From the clouds droop gilded chariots and the white forms of angels."[2]

The Black Crook filled the coffers of the three impresarios to overflowing, setting them up financially for life. It also alerted other New York producers to the financial benefits of the spectacular and set the stage for some of the most extravagant shows in New York history—*Ziegfeld Follies*.

Florenz Ziegfeld, Jr., discovered show business at the age of fourteen, when *Buffalo Bill's Wild West Show* came to his hometown of Chicago. He determined the stage was his calling, and ten years later he produced his first *Follies of 1907: Glorifying the American Girl*. Fifty stunning chorus girls paraded about the stage in a collection of musical numbers and scenes. It played in New York for the summer, then toured.

The box office receipts for this spectacular were so substantial that Ziegfeld determined to better it the next season. This time he included his name in the title, and with this second production, *Ziegfeld Follies* became a Broadway institution with new editions year after year.

But growing up alongside these lavish spectaculars was their polar opposite: the sparsely produced vaudeville show. It became the most popular form of entertainment in the United States in the late 1900s. Vaudeville offered a wide variety of specialty acts: singing, juggling, magic, and animal acts as well as dancing. Think of it as the *America's Got Talent* of its day. At first, the dancing consisted of acrobatic solos, comedic sketches, and eccentric contortionist acts like that of Ray Bolger, best remembered for his later performance as the Scarecrow in the MGM movie *The Wizard of Oz*.

Tap was a big hit on the vaudeville circuits. Bill "Bojangles" Robinson is credited as the founding father of tap dancing. As a teenager, he began performing in the pickaninny chorus (a group of black children) in the minstrel show *The South Before the War*. He moved to New York in 1900 and teamed up with another black dancer, George W. Cooper. Each performer had wanted to work the Keith and Orpheum vaudeville circuits, but there was a "two colored" rule at that time that would only allow black artists to perform if they were seen in pairs. So the two men became a duo. Fifteen years later, however, Robinson had become the only black solo act in vaudeville. He was a dynamic performer, virtually impossible to top. Though he was usually slated second on the bill, more often than not, Robinson ended up performing last. No one wanted to follow his act.

 SPOTLIGHT

Gregory Hines: The Definition of the Triple Threat

Gregory Hines was a true triple threat, performing in movies like *White Nights*, alongside legendary Mikhail Baryshnikov, and on Broadway in *Sophisticated Ladies*. He was an innovator in the art of tap, not only keeping it alive, but expanding it for future generations.

Hines began training in tap at the age of three with Henry LeTang. At five, Hines and his older brother, Maurice, began touring the world, dancing in nightclubs and on television as *The Hines Kids*. Their dad joined the act as their drummer, and the act became *Hines, Hines, and Dad*.

Later in his career, Hines worked again with Maurice in the Broadway show *Eubie!* and with his first teacher, Henry LeTang, as choreographer. His performance earned him his first Tony nomination.

He actually won the award at a later date for his work in *Jelly's Last Jam*. Hines was a strong supporter of the inauguration of National Tap Day (May 25) and a supporter of the first Los Angeles Tap Festival.

As vaudeville began to fade, Robinson performed in several Broadway shows. By the 1930s, he was working in Hollywood in such films as *The Little Colonel* and *Stormy Weather*.

This cross-pollination of dance talent brings up a question: does Hollywood borrow from Broadway, or does Broadway borrow from Hollywood? The answer is: yes!

It began with *42nd Street*. In 1932, America was deep into The Great Depression, hardly a time to put a lighthearted musical into production. But producer Darryl F. Zanuck pressured Warner Bros. Studios to do exactly that. The film would use musical veterans and introduce newcomer Ruby Keeler. Directing was the wizard of kaleidoscopic overhead shots and spectacular production numbers, Busby Berkeley. *42nd Street* proved to be the medicine the country needed to chase away the Depression blues. With musical numbers like "Lullaby of Broadway" and "We're in the Money" and Ruby Keeler tap dancing away atop a taxi cab in the title song "42nd Street," an audience couldn't help but feel better—at least for ninety minutes. Hollywood had found the perfect antidote to the country's troubles.

As a reaction to Warner's success with *42nd Street*, RKO Pictures decided to produce its own Hollywood musical showcase, *Flying Down to Rio*. It used Hollywood starlet Ginger Rogers as the wisecracking, dancing ingénue, and a new Broadway talent was brought in to partner her—Fred Astaire.

Thus, the legendary Fred Astaire–Ginger Rogers partnership was launched, which is truly the best part of the otherwise unmemorable *Rio*. Astaire partnered other talented dancers throughout his movie career, including Cyd Charisse, Vera Ellen, and Joan Crawford. His competition tap number with Eleanor Powell in *Broadway Melody* is a showcase of both style and precision. But something clicked with Rogers. As a dance team, Astaire and Rogers became highly bankable stars. Hollywood continued to crank out movie musical after movie musical throughout the Depression era, and the box office was never better.

Astaire himself is the definition of elegance. His graceful ease in *Top Hat* still influences dancers today, like ABT principal ballet dancer David Hallberg. "I was glued to the way he moved, his seamless way of movement. He was a huge inspiration to me."[3]

Just over the horizon and rapidly gaining ground was jazz. Originally a "dance of the people," jazz dance is rooted in jazz music—African music and rhythms punctuated by syncopation. Jack Cole is credited with introducing jazz to American dance. Cole developed the first permanent dance ensemble for a movie studio. While working for Columbia Pictures, Cole trained such legendary greats as Gwen Verdon, Matt Maddox, and Carole Haney. Cole was tough and his technique was difficult, requiring almost superhuman stamina. But he got results.

While Hollywood had been focusing on glamour, tinsel, and absolutely nothing serious, the Broadway musical had begun to explore more dramatic elements. *On Your Toes*, with music and lyrics by Richard Rogers and Lorenz Hart, was originally produced in 1936 and choreographed by George Balanchine (yes, *that* George Balanchine). The story takes place backstage at a ballet company and includes a clever comic parody of the Ballets Russes production of *Scheherazade* (who would know better how to stage that send-up than Balanchine?). *On Your Toes* not only integrated the dancing with the plot, it became essential to the plot.

The finale of the show is the famous "Slaughter on Tenth Avenue" ballet. The hero (originally played be Ray Bolger) has to keep dancing or risk being shot. Dancing was no longer performed as a diversion; it helped tell the story. *On Your Toes* threw down the gauntlet where

Broadway dancing was concerned by raising the standard and holding back the curtain for more seriously themed musicals.

Accepting the challenge was Agnes de Mille's choreography for the 1943 blockbuster *Oklahoma!* Classically trained in ballet, de Mille not only drilled her dancers on the steps, she schooled them in acting as well. (Her uncle was the famous early Hollywood film director, Cecil B. de Mille). Broadway now had a new breed of choreographer. "The Dream Ballet" that ends Act I expresses the lead character's concerns and desires as to which of two men she will ultimately choose. As the dance sequence progresses, the dream turns into a nightmare, and the "real" woman awakes, shaken. Not only did *Oklahoma!* revolutionize Broadway dancing, it revolutionized the Broadway musical by using dance to express the thoughts and feelings of the central characters. In addition, the show did not open with the traditional "bring on the dancing girls" production number. Instead, it opened with a lone cowboy singing a ballad! "No girls, no kicks, no show" had been the production philosophy of the Broadway musical comedy; *Oklahoma!* changed all of that.

The Big Three—Robbins, Champion, and Fosse

Jerome Robbins took de Mille's ideas even further. Like Balanchine, Robbins was a well-trained ballet dancer who could move fluidly from choreographing a classical ballet to staging a number for a Broadway musical. His work in musical theater ranges from the childlike, delightful, and clever dances for *Peter Pan* to the gritty, violent yet graceful feuds between two rival street gangs in *West Side Story*. It is Robbins's work in *West Side Story* that turned the corner for the American musical. (It later became a successful movie musical.) As director/choreographer, Robbins expertly blended dance, movement, staging, acting, comedy, and drama into one seamless whole. He elevated the position of choreographer from second-string stager of musical numbers to being the driving force of a musical.

It is also with *West Side Story* that the Broadway musical came of age. Once it was dealing with serious themes and drama, the Broadway show was no longer musical comedy; it had evolved into American musical theater.

LOCATION, LOCATION, LOCATION

The location shots for the film of *West Side Story* were done in New York City. The Sharks and the Jets danced through the streets of Manhattan in (what was then) slums, just before the buildings were torn down to build one of New York's cultural landmarks, Lincoln Center.

Back across the country, Hollywood had now entered the golden age of musicals. The movies and the performances made during this period are classics, still holding up as quality work decades after they were released. The figure of Gene Kelly swinging from a lamppost in *Singin' in the Rain* is the iconic image of this era. But Kelly wasn't the only dancing star. Some of the best dancers of this time are immortalized on film, including Jaques D'Ambois, Tommy Rahl, Matt Maddox, Russ Tamblin, Donald O'Connor, Cyd Charisse, Shirley MacLaine, Gwen Verdon, Bob Fosse, and Marge and Gower Champion.

The elegant and classy dance team of Marge and Gower Champion was well known from their work in their own TV show as well as movies for MGM such as *Lovely to Look At* and *Showboat*. With a well-established film career as a dancer, Gower moved into the role of director/choreographer at MGM. But his heart was really on Broadway. The Tony (Antoinette Perry) Award–winning shows *Carnival*; *Bye, Bye Birdie*; *Hello, Dolly!*; and *42nd Street* are all stellar examples of Gower Champion's directorial vision as well as choreographic inventiveness. Champion focused

Name: Craig Blakeney
Job: Dancer

When did you start dancing and why?

When I first went to college at the Shenandoah Conservatory in Virginia, I had to take some dance classes and I was surprised that I placed above first level in ballet. I had no terminology; I had no formal training. I thought I needed to be in a level 1 class, but the teacher forced me to stay in the higher class *and* learn the terminology. There was also a jazz teacher who had been on Broadway. When she was pregnant, she had me demonstrate for her classes. Now, in New York, I go to dance calls, and that's how I work. I am unbelievably thankful for my training in college.

What was your first big decision?

When, I graduated from college, I [decided to go] directly to New York. It's a little tricky with my skill set. The shows I do are more classic. [But] I go to see shows, and . . . friends with whom I have worked are in them. The more shows you do, the more people know you.

What's next?

I want to work with kids. When I am finished performing, I would love to teach in a musical theater department— teach a choreography class, stage movement, acting class . . . all of these aspects.

on the connectivity among the acting, singing and dancing in his shows. "I use dancing to embellish, extend, or enlarge upon an existing emotion," he said in an interview with the *New York Times*. "None of it could really stand alone. Being director and choreographer is the same; one concept that you try to fold in so there is a constant flow."[4]

Champion wanted his shows to *move* seamlessly from one scene to another. Not willing to use the artificial crossover or "number in one" done in front of a scrim or curtain to cover a scenery change, Champion choreographed his set changes with the same amount of intricacy and attention to detail that he used when choreographing his dance numbers. More often than not, the dancers and principals assisted with the set changes. In Champion's revival of *Annie Get Your Gun*, he flew the set pieces and stripped the stage bare of all props, leaving only a blue cyclorama so that his dancers would have full use of the stage to perform the "There's No Business Like Show Business" number in Act I. Originally done as a "number in one" with three actors, Champion transformed the song into his ". . . valentine to show business"[5] expanding it into a highly inventive, show-stopping dance sequence using all his dancers to represent the many different characters who populate the wonderful world of show business. Like Robbins, Champion focused on the individuality of his dancers; he didn't want them to "blend." He used their uniqueness to give dimension to his productions.

An admirer of Champion's work as both dancer and choreographer, Bob Fosse also launched his career as a dance team. Originally partnered with Marian Niles as "Fosse and Niles," Fosse introduced the dancing duo to the elite audience at the Pierre Hotel's Cotillion Room in New York as, "You've heard of Marge and Gower Champion? Well, we're the runner-ups."[6] Ironically, when Fosse arrived on the MGM lot at the age of twenty-two, he and Champion worked together in the film, *Give a Girl a Break*, in which Champion played the director/choreographer of a Broadway show and Fosse played his assistant.

As the golden-haired boy wonder, Fosse danced in some of the great—and not so great—MGM movie musicals. He was one of the suitors in MGM's production of *Kiss Me, Kate*. Hermes Pan choreographed the movie, but Fosse choreographed his duet with Carol Haney in the "Tom, Dick, or Harry" number. The difference between Pan's choreography and Fosse's was more than obvious and marked the beginning of the Fosse style. This short sequence brought him to the attention of Broadway producers. Returning to New York, Fosse choreographed his first Broadway show, *The Pajama Game*, at the age of twenty-three. It was a huge hit, and it won the Tony Awards for Best Musical and Best Choreography for the 1954 season. Fosse's career as a choreographer was launched and went on to include such Broadway shows and movies as *Damn Yankees* (stage and film), *How to Succeed in Business Without Really Trying, Sweet Charity* (stage and film), *Chicago* (stage), *Pippin* (stage), *Dancin'* (stage), and his last work, the autobiographical film, *All That Jazz*. In 1973, Fosse became the only director/choreographer to have won the show business "Triple Crown"—a Tony (*Pippin*, Broadway), an Emmy (*Liza With a 'Z'*, television), and an Oscar (*Cabaret*, film).

These three men—Robbins, Champion, and Fosse—ushered American musical theater into its Golden Age. It is due to their creative efforts that the Broadway musical evolved into a cohesive whole, the vision of one master, the director/choreographer.

A generation later, Michael Bennett turned Broadway musical theater upside down and inside out by making the star of his show the chorus dancer. Bennett received his first Tony nomination at the age of twenty-three for *A Joyful Noise*. He was quoted as saying, "Dance is the essence of the Broadway musical. What I want to do is to make the movement give a psychological insight into a character, to advance the story and make a point quickly."[7] Bennett had staged three musicals when he decided he wanted to do a musical about dancers.

On January 18, 1974, after the curtains had come down for the night on all the musicals then running on Broadway, Bennett sat down in a dance studio with twenty-one other dancers to talk about and record the stories of their lives. This was the beginning of a two-year workshop which would end in a significant show in musical theater history—*A Chorus Line*.

Center Stage
profile

Name: John Williford
Job: Dancer

When did you start dancing and why?

I was a vocal major, but my girlfriend took me to a college dance audition. There were sixty girls and only three guys—the odds were good. I always loved to dance; I just didn't think I had the aptitude for it. I owe most of my career to that program.

What was your first big decision?

After I graduated, I did six months on a cruise ship. Then I had a college roommate in Los Angeles, [where] I thought there might be more opportunities. I wanted to try television and film. I ended up doing a lot of regional musical theater; then *Starlight Express* in Las Vegas, and then in Germany. It was the most extreme show I had ever been in, physically and mentally. You really have to up your game. The triple threat is more blended than before. Dancers think differently than everyone else. We're the ones who do what no one else will do. We're the ones who go through the pain. We do this because we have to. It's what we love.

What's next?

I have already been working in video editing, and photography.

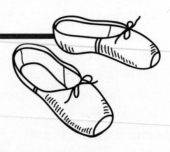

WORD SEARCH

Movie Musical Word Search

Can you find six or more Broadway shows that went on to became a movie musical? (There are fifteen total.) Be sure to look in all directions.

```
H R Y V C A I O D T Q C A U R F U W
Y I G N E A C H I C A G O E B D G G
R T D J U B R F J G G W W T K H M A
O R L N B G E O I Z O O Y G O E D O
T N R O A M R V U C O T G S L L O H
S Y I K B G Y U X S I U L K B L L M
E N G L V S N F O R E K W M N O I C
D J Y A V Q L I A Y Z L N G H D V U
I E N H S T V H K I T R O A D O E Q
S V N O I B C R K E R E S N K L R P
T H U M V T B I J H H L G N Q L Y E
S R F A E W W S A D F T A E O Y Y T
E Q A E B Y E B Y E B I R D I E R B
W S W V F G R M E K E X V F Y N H W
Q S T H E P A J A M A G A M E A N K
N H C P U Z Q B B N G U O T G A Z A
J D H S T H E M U S I C M A N T F K
N L N M B E S O U T H P A C I F I C
```

ANNIE GET YOUR GUN • BYE, BYE BIRDIE • CAROUSEL • CHICAGO
FUNNY GIRL • HELLO, DOLLY! • THE KING AND I • THE MUSIC MAN
MY FAIR LADY • OKLAHOMA! • OLIVER • THE PAJAMA GAME
SOUTH PACIFIC • SWEET CHARITY • WEST SIDE STORY

THE GYPSY ROBE

Dancers in Broadway shows refer to themselves as gypsies because they continually travel from show to show to show. These gypsies have a tradition involving the Gypsy Robe, which is an actual dressing gown passed on from one Broadway company to the next. The oldest dancer from the most recent show to open on Broadway ceremonially presents the robe onstage to the chorus dancer with the most Broadway credits in the show that is about to give its opening night performance. After receiving the robe, each company sews its emblem on it. When the robe is completely covered in various show emblems, a new robe is put into circulation. The completed Gypsy Robes from across the decades, dating back to 1950, are housed at the New York Public Library for the Performing Arts, the Smithsonian Institute, and the Actors' Equity Association headquarters.

In the Wings
profile

Name: Liliana Wicoxson
Age: 17
Job (when not studying!): Dance student
Dream Job: Absolutely, hands down, I'd have to say my dream job would be working on Broadway. Dancing, acting, and singing, doing everything I love.

When did you start dancing and why?
I was three. I started at Ballet Academy East in New York. When my family moved to Los Angeles, I studied only tap. I really didn't focus on dancing until I was eleven. Not doing

ballet for three years set me back. Without ballet, you don't have anything.

Why did you audition for Los Angeles Ballet Academy?
All the girls there were so passionate about ballet. I learned so much being around people like that. It really gave me the drive to get better. [I realized] if I don't get my act together, I won't be able to do what I love.

How do you feel about dancing in Broadway musicals?
When I was six, I did musicals and I fell in love with it.

How do you fit school into all of this?
I have straight *A*s. I could totally have an academic career if I wanted to.

What about your social life?
I have definitely made a lot of sacrifices—birthday parties, hanging out with friends. A lot of my friends used to be dancers, but they didn't have the dedication.

What are your plans after high school?
I am applying to fifteen different colleges with musical theater programs. I would like to go to an East Coast school so I can audition and live in New York.

Get There from Here

There is only one way to a Broadway stage, and that is the audition.

Research Upcoming Auditions
You will find auditions listed in *Backstage*, the trade publication that comes out once a week. Calls for Broadway, summer stock,

regional theater, industrials, and others are listed in *Backstage*. Similar to auditioning for a ballet company or a contemporary company, you show up at a specific place, warm up, and are ready to dance at a specific time. Many Broadway auditions are held at Broadway theaters in addition to rehearsal halls. There are two calls: one for union members (Actors' Equity Association, AEA) and the nonunion call. The nonunion call will generally have more people attending than the union call, but be prepared; you will easily be competing against two hundred dancers at the union call for a Broadway show.

Prepare for the Audition

As part of the audition, you will be given dance combinations to do. Generally, a ballet combination is first, as it quickly tells the choreographer what your level of training is. The first cut is made, and the number of people auditioning are reduced easily by 50 percent or more. A jazz combination is next. The choreographer is looking to see how fast you pick up both the steps and

the style. Another cut is made, and the field is usually narrowed down to twenty dancers; these are the finalists. It is not uncommon to call back the finalists for another round of auditioning at another time, a day or a week or so later. It is also possible that the decision will be made the first day. It just depends on the production.

You will be asked to sing at some point, so be prepared with an up-tempo piece and a ballad that suit your voice and show your range. You should have your music with you, and it should be in the correct key.

Dress the Part

When you dress for a Broadway audition, you want to look professional. As a general rule, you don't want to look like a ballet dancer, nor do you want to look like you just stepped off the street in hip-hop garb—unless, of course, you are auditioning for a show that has those specific requirements. You will want to wear something with a contemporary, jazzy kind of look that lends itself to versatility.

Psych Yourself Up!

The psychology of auditioning is very important. All you can ask of yourself is to do the best you can. There are going to be some really good dancers on that stage. You must focus on your own performance at the audition and ask yourself afterward if you were happy with the work you did. So much goes into casting that has absolutely nothing to do with your talent or ability. If you don't get this job, don't take it personally. Just think ahead to the next audition. As you make the rounds, you will find that the same people show up at every audition, and it generally narrows down to the same few. If you are making the cuts, you will eventually be one of those chosen few.

Keep On Keepin' On

Even when you have a job, you should continue to audition just to keep your competitive edge.

AVOIDING THE PITFALLS OF DOWNTIME

In every dancer's career, there is some downtime, either scheduled (when you are with a company and it is the off season) or unscheduled (if you are a commercial dancer hip-hopping from one music video to another, or if you are on a tour). Your body does need some rest from time to time, but you also need to keep dancing to stay fit for your return to class, rehearsal, and performance—or there won't be a return. The answer to the situation is cross-training by participating in physical activities that complement your dancing.

Pilates is a great exercise program for dancers. You will find a good number of dancers incorporate Pilates exercises into their routine warm-ups. Pilates works from your core or center and focuses on building strength through flexibility.

Yoga is another alternative. Mind Body Dancer is a system of yoga specifically designed as cross-training exercises for dancers. "Yoga is about learning the differences between discomfort, challenge and injury. It's awakening patience and learning to let go."[8]

Swimming is another good way to cross-train. It, too, emphasizes lengthening and stretching the muscles. The body is buoyant in the water and works in zero gravity, which allows muscles and joints to relax. Swimming also increases stamina, improves flexibility, and is an excellent way to rehabilitate after an injury.

4

Get with the Times: Contemporary, Modern, and Hip-Hop

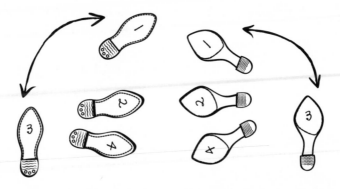

Contemporary dance is a combination of classical ballet and modern dance. Classical ballet gives it structure, modern dance takes that structure and either uses it or refuses it.

Modern dance began to emerge at the beginning of the twentieth century. It was started by two American "revolutionaries" on opposite sides of the country: the independent-minded Isadora Duncan on the West Coast and Ruth St. Denis on the East Coast. Although Isadora and Ruth each struck out on two different paths, they both wanted the same thing: to interpret dance on their own terms. Isadora would eventually be known as the Mother of Modern Dance and Ruth, the First Lady of American Dance.

Mother of Modern Dance

Duncan began her professional career at age eighteen with a Chicago touring company. One year later, she moved to New York, hoping to further her career. To continue her training, she took ballet lessons with the ballerina Maria Bonfanti, famed for her performances in the five-hour spectacular *The Black Crook*. (Since they were both in New York at the same time and both studied with the same teacher, it is thought that Isadora Duncan and Ruth St. Denis may have actually taken class together!) Frustrated when she discovered that female dancers in New York were limited to being showgirls and that ballet refused to stray from its strict, codified technique, Duncan set off for Europe to find a more suitable environment for her type of dance.

When Duncan arrived in Paris in 1900, her free-form interpretation of Indian and Asian dance created quite a stir. She based her dances on improvisation and natural movements, like running and skipping. Nothing was structured. She defined her work as, "the highest intelligence in the freest body,"[1] and she became the talk of the artistic elite in all the chic salons of Paris.

With the first modern Olympic Games in 1901, everything considered Greek became fashionable. So Duncan took off her Victorian corset and costumed herself in flowing tunics resembling the clothing of the ancient Greeks. (Sounds a lot like Marie Sallé, doesn't it?) When Mikhail Fokine, Russian choreographer for the Ballets Russes, saw her dance in Paris, he found Duncan's expressive performance to be his source of inspiration for two of his ballets, *Les Sylphides* and *The Dying Swan*, as performed by Anna Pavlova. Vaslav Nijinsky, however, was unimpressed, stating that without technique, there could be no art. But Duncan was forming her own new technique. Her influence can be seen in the work of today's contemporary choreographers, such as Mark Morris and José Limón.

First Lady of American Dance

At the same time, at the opposite end of the country, a farm girl from Newark, New Jersey, was making her own discoveries. Like Duncan, Ruth St. Denis, had next to no formal training. She was what could be called an "instinctive dancer." She had a certain natural ability, ". . . a line of conduct I have followed ever since,"[2] she said. Perhaps because she was raised on a farm, St. Denis was not only physically connected to nature by her family's lifestyle but found its motions to be the source of inspiration for her dances. The rolling waves of the ocean as they crashed upon the shore, the stirring of grass in the wind. However, her first steps into the theatrical world were not so organic. Her career actually began in the rather raucous world of vaudeville.

Accompanied by her mother, the teenage St. Denis simply showed up in the foyer of a variety house on Sixth Avenue in New York City and declared that she would like to audition. With no formal training, her "dance" was really a series of acrobatic tricks—high kicks, backbends, and splits—nothing unusual for the order of the day. By her own admission, it wasn't "what I did but for the way I did it"[3] that won her a spot on the bill, eleven performances a day.

The vaudeville house launched her career. She was seen by a theatrical agent who started arranging bookings for her, one of which was *Zaza* for famed director David Belasco. (It was Balasco who inserted the "St." into her name.) In an instant, she was off to London. She spent the next five years working as an actress in Belasco shows in Europe as well as touring the United States. But it wasn't until she stumbled upon an Egyptian-themed poster for cigarettes that she received the urge, the inspiration, and the need to return to dance. She conceived of a project she called *Egypta*, but she was not able to launch it until six years later, in 1910.

During that time, she studied both Asian and Indian dance and designed a solo production for herself entitled *Rahda*. Then it was back to the vaudeville houses with this seventeen-minute solo ballet, which was sandwiched in between a boxer and a monkey act. The advertising for her dance stated, "The entire dance will be performed in bare feet."[4] That novelty attracted much attention, and a new career exhibiting a new style of "Eastern dance" was born in America.

Her great success with *Rhada* in 1906 made the next step for St. Denis very clear: Europe. Ruth St. Denis became the talk of Paris. She was also highly praised in Germany and Austria. St. Denis returned to the United States as a celebrated artist. After one of her performances in Boston, Philip Hale, one of the country's foremost music critics at the time, stated, "In comparing the dancing of Ruth St. Denis, the posturing, the prancing, the loping, the bounding of Isadora Duncan seem common and material." He went on, that "[St. Denis's] body is that of a woman divinely planned . . . a picture of beauty never to be forgotten."[5]

In 1914, a young dancer named Ted Shawn became one of St. Denis's students. He also became her husband. Together, they were involved in the creation of the legendary Jacob's Pillow Dance Festival. They also founded the Denishawn School of Dancing and Related Arts, the "cradle of American dance." Some of the company members included Doris Humphrey, Charles Weidman, and that incomparable revolutionary Martha Graham.

The Family Tree

St. Denis Led to Graham

Martha Graham is frequently credited with bringing dance into the twentieth century. Her influence has been compared to that of Igor Stravinsky's on music. She was born in Pennsylvania in 1894. When she was fourteen, her father moved the family across the country to Santa Barbara, California. After high school, she began her dance studies at the Denishawn School located in Los Angeles. But neither Ruth St. Denis nor Ted Shawn thought that Graham had the ability to become a dancer. So Graham practiced alone in the dark at two o'clock in the morning, making up her own movements so that "when the time came for me to dance, I would be ready."[6]

She was given her chance with *Serenata Morisca*, a Moorish dance choreographed by Ted Shawn. Graham was allowed to teach the dance but was not considered capable of performing it. When the lead dancer of the Denishawn company fell ill, Graham immediately asked for the solo. She performed the solo on the spot and the rest is history.

Graham danced with Denishawn for seven years, then left in 1926 to form her own dance company in New York. The Martha Graham Center of Contemporary Dance is the oldest dance company in America.

Ten years later, she choreographed *Chronicle*, the work that would define her as her own artist and revolutionize dance in the process. Dealing with serious themes, it turned a corner for modern dance as to purpose and expression. The other work for which she is well-known is *Appalachian Spring*, set to a score by Aaron Copland.

Graham's influence paved the way for Merce Cunningham, Paul Taylor, and many other modern dancers. Each in turn has had their own influence on American dance, creating a bridge from its early modern phase to the contemporary dance that began to emerge in the 1950s.

Graham Led to Cunningham

Merce Cunningham was invited to join Martha Graham's company after she saw him dance in Seattle. He spent the next six years in Graham's company as a soloist, then became a teacher at Black Mountain College. It was here that he formed the Merce Cunningham Dance Company with the purpose of exploring new ideas in dance and technology. The original company consisted of six dancers, two musicians, and a stage manager touring the country all crammed into a Volkswagen bus. (Sounds a bit like the start of the Joffrey, doesn't it?)

Cunningham's most revolutionary idea dealt with the relationship between dance and music. He experimented with the two being created separately rather than working in collaboration. (Kind of retro—all the way back to the dances of medieval Europe, that is.) Similar to George Balanchine and the New York City Ballet, Cunningham did away with any kind of dramatic arc or storytelling preferring the existence of dance for movement alone.

Cunningham Led to Taylor

Paul Taylor was one of the original six Cunningham dancers. A strong and lyrical soloist, he had danced in Graham's company and had also worked with Balanchine. After the first year with Cunningham's company, Taylor formed his own Paul Taylor Dance Company in New York City in 1954. Taylor could be considered the innovator who began to merge ballet with modern method to create today's contemporary dance. His work ranges from playful and exuberant to desperate and edgy. Solid training is needed to perform his choreography.

Taylor Led to Tharp

Twyla Tharp danced with Paul Taylor's company for two years before starting her own company. (Do you see the pattern here?) When Robert Joffrey wanted something fresh and original for The Joffrey Ballet, he hired Tharp to choreograph *Deuce Coupe*. Tharp's work in *Deuce Coupe* is full-on classical ballet working opposite full-on rock and roll, and it launched her career.

Adding to the Mix

Mexican dancer José Limón formed his New York dance company in 1946 after having served in the US Army in World War II. The Limón Dance Company celebrated its sixty-fifth year in 2012 and has made a substantial contribution to the development of modern dance in the United States. The company balances Hispanic heritage with works of contemporary choreographers. It was the first cultural ambassador appointed by the US State Department to represent the United States in other countries. It was also the first dance company invited to perform at the New York State Theater (now known as the David H. Koch Theater) when Lincoln Center opened in 1964. Limón's choreography for his company was driven by his passion and spontaneity. And he gave dimension to the dance by sometimes working against the music. Limón himself was praised as being "the finest male dancer of his time" by the *New York Times*.[7]

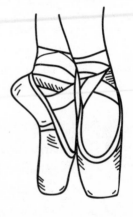

Dating from its first performance at the Ninety-Second Street YMCA in New York City in 1958, the Alvin Ailey American Dance Theater also revolutionized the thinking of dance in the United States. Ailey was born in Texas in 1931, then moved to California at the age of twelve. He was first exposed to dance on a school field trip to see the Ballet Russe de Monte Carlo. He began his formal training shortly thereafter.

Ailey studied with Lester Horton, founder of the first racially integrated dance company in the United States, and launched his dance career with Horton's company. Ailey was invited to dance on Broadway in *House of Flowers* and went on to create his own dance company. Since then, the Alvin Ailey American Dance Theater has toured seventy-one countries on six continents and has been named "a vital American cultural ambassador to the world"[8] by the US Congress.

Lil Buck:
Jookin' Star and Classics Friend

Memphis, Tennessee, put a different spin on hip-hop with the development of jookin'. Think hip-hop with a Southern accent; the sound is particular and the rhythms are different. Jookin' started as a walking step accented by a sharp lifting of the knees. Then gliding was added, along with the usual popping and waving. But then came—are you ready for this?—pointe work in tennis shoes! This includes prolonged balances as well as multiple turns (and turns in attitude), all on pointe. And this is being done by guys, one of the most notable being Lil Buck, aka Charles Riley.

It is the rare dancer who can jump from jookin' on the streets of Memphis to a concert with renowned cellist Yo-Yo Ma. Nonetheless, that is the story of Lil Buck, who can also claim a close association with former NYCB principal dancer Damian Woetzel.

After learning some new moves from his sister, Charles Riley took to jookin' at the Crystal Palace, a skating rink in Memphis. He started creating his own moves; and at seventeen, when he was rehearsing with his hip-hop crew at a local ballet school, he was offered a scholarship by the school's owner. Through his exposure to ballet, he developed his own version of *The Dying Swan*, which has become his signature solo. It was filmed and put on YouTube, where Woetzel saw it. Woetzel in turn showed the video to Yo-Yo Ma, and ultimately, the famed cellist and jookin' dancer performed together at (Le) Poisson Rouge in New York (viewed over one million times on YouTube). Lil Buck also performed *The Dying Swan* at the Youth America Grand Prix, dancing in tandem with ballerina Nina Ananiashvili—his version alongside her performance of the original choreography by Fokine.

Name: Nicholas Duran
Job: Dancer

When did you start dancing and why?
I was originally trained as a gymnast. I was at a performing arts middle school in Tucson, Arizona, and I wanted to get out of PE. In high school I auditioned for jazz and took ballet at the . . . Ballet Arts [Foundation]. I was fourteen [and] in with a bunch of eleven- and twelve-year-old girls! I went to the University of Arizona as a dance major. It was wonderful but hard.

What is the difference between contemporary and commercial dance?
The audiences are different. The audience for concert dance is more sophisticated. Also, the pay scales are different—commercial pays more. But a contemporary dance career has greater longevity. Commercial is more driven by fads; there is no technique involved. You never see a commercial dancer in a contemporary class.

What was your first big decision?
After college, I moved to Chicago. I decided to audition for the Luna Negra Dance Theater. I was late to the audition. You

were supposed to be on the list, but they let me go in anyway to take the barre. They had more dancers than they expected; they cut people then divided us into two groups. We did center work, then they cut again. After that, they took us into a smaller room, and we did rep [work from the company's choreographic repertory]. They cut again, down to eight dancers, only two guys. Then they took us individually into a smaller room. That's when they told me I had the job. The odds were 110 to 1.

What's next?
My backup is teaching fitness. I am already teaching yoga and would like to have a fitness program for celebrity clients.

Get There from Here

By now you have realized that just as you must audition to get a position in a ballet company, you must audition for a contemporary company. As you can see from Nick Duran's story, contemporary dance is just as competitive as ballet or Broadway. As one Paul Taylor dancer put it, "For the women, you can have as many as three hundred auditions—not for the company, just for one position."[9]

STATE OF THE (DANCE) UNION

In the United States, the professional ballet world operates in cooperation with the American Guild of Musical Artists (AGMA). This union also governs concert dance, opera singers, and musicians. While some of the smaller companies do not work with the union, the larger ones do. The union negotiates contracts with the various companies, and these contracts determine your pay scale, working conditions, and length of rehearsal periods. It is also called into service to resolve disputes between the artists and the management. There are different contracts to suit the needs of companies depending on the company's size, types of touring venues, frequency of performances, etc. If you are hired by a professional ballet company that is a part of the union, you will be asked to join the union. There are initiation fees and annual dues, but these are usually taken out of your paycheck in small amounts.

The Taft/Hartley Law prevents unions from forcing you to join on your first job. After that one time, however, you will have to join. If you want a career as a professional dancer, join the AGMA as soon as you have your first professional job. All the performing unions work in cooperation with each other, offering discounted initiation fees to new members who already belong to one or more of its sister unions.

Love Your Fit Body

All contemporary dancers are well trained with wonderfully athletic bodies. The contemporary dancer is not trying to compete with the sylph. Muscular, well-toned, and resilient is the "look" of the contemporary world. It also includes different heights and is more forgiving of different body structures. For example, a terrific female dancer who is too tall for the ballet world can fully use all her classical training in a contemporary company. The same thing applies to a male dancer who is shorter or taller or broader than what is desired in ballet.

Follow What the Group Does

If you are interested in working in a contemporary company, research them online, watch their videos on YouTube, and rent their DVDs. This research will help you narrow the field as to which companies would be a good fit for you. Just as you would if you were auditioning for a ballet company, study what the dancers wear for class and rehearsal, then select something similar to wear at your audition. You will definitely want to choose an outfit that is simple and illustrates your line. While you need to have solid classical training to do contemporary work, you don't want to walk in to a contemporary audition looking like a ballet dancer.

Start Small

In most cases, you will need to physically go to a company's base of operations to audition or to a designated city where they will be holding auditions. If you are not already living in New York, Los Angeles, or Chicago, you will find that each of these three cities will present you with its own brand of culture shock. Not to worry—you will adjust. A good way to give yourself a leg up on the feel of a company and the city in which it is located is to take a summer intensive program offered by that company. Yes, you will have to audition for most summer programs, but that is good practice for a career that is fueled by auditioning. The stakes aren't nearly as high when you are auditioning for a summer program as they are when you are auditioning for a job. The intensive programs usually last between three and five weeks and will give you some exposure to the teachers, choreographers, and repertory of the company.

You will also discover that there is a big difference between the East Coast and the West Coast dancer. According to *So You Think You Can Dance* choreographer Stacey Tookey, "There is a really strong work ethic and training focus on the East Coast, whereas dancers train a bit more sporadically on the West Coast. LA is full of commercial jobs that are short gigs . . . In New York, there are a lot more long-term jobs like company work and Broadway."[10] You need to be aware of and understand this difference if you are going to work in either town.

GOODWILL DANCERS

The United States Bureau of Educational and Cultural Affairs (BECA) has been inviting American dance companies to tour around the world as cultural emissaries since the program began in 2010. One of these, the contemporary ballet troupe the Sean Curran Company, visited China, South Korea, the Philippines, and Vietnam. The purpose was not only to perform but to initiate a cultural exchange through outreach activities with the various communities where the company performed. The company's choreographer, Trey McIntyre, whose work has been described as "a classic slice of Americana,"[11] was also charged with selecting an international company to come to the United States as part of the exchange.

This is not the first time in recent history that dance has been used as a cultural ambassador to ease political tensions around the world. In 1960, at the height of the Cold War, dance emissaries were sent to the Soviet Block, with the legendary dance team of Marge and Gower Champion among them. Let's think back to the origin of formal dance and how it was used to ease the friction between France and Italy. By now, you have probably noticed history has a habit of repeating itself. Clearly, Catherine de Medici had a good idea.

Hip-Hop

Hip-hop is the dancing you see in the music videos of Eminem, Justin Timberlake, Rhianna, and Katy Perry. You see it on television commercials, like those advertising cars and electronic tablets. Reality shows like *So You Think You Can Dance* have featured dancers like tWitch. All dance is a form of self-expression, and hip-hop has not only expanded upon that idea, it has taken it to a whole new level.

History of Hip-Hop

The term *hip-hop* is a combination of an old African-American slang term *hip*, meaning "current" or "with it," and *hop*, referring to the hopping movement of the dance as it was first performed. Originating in the South Bronx of New York City, hip-hop started as street dancing performed at block parties and parks. DJ Kool Herc is considered the father of hip-hop. He would plug the amps for his speakers into the lampposts at 163rd and Prospect Avenue, and using two turntables, play records looping certain rhythmic patterns of the music, called "breaks." This "juggling" led to rap music, rhythmic chanting in sixteen-bar phrases, and beatboxing, a percussive use of the human voice to simulate drum machines and emphasize certain rhythmic elements of the music.

Over the last four decades, hip-hop has borrowed freely from soul music, funk, and rhythm and blues. The rapped lyrics originally expressed the frustrations of urban ghetto life. In more recent years, however, hip-hop has moved into the mainstream, and the words have crossed over to more standard themes. The songs are still performed to an ultra percussive beat at uber-loud decibel levels.

Break It Down

Today's hip-hop has many diverse styles or techniques that, like any form of dance, are determined by the individual choreographers working in the medium and how they apply them. The different styles of hip hop are:

Breaking: Named for the break in the music where the dancer can show off his/her best moves.

Floor work: Like windmills (balancing on one shoulder), has become iconic in representing the art form.

Popping: Smooth body movements, such as the undulating body wave or worm on the floor.

Locking: Angular movements in isolation, such as a single hand movement or pointing.

Jookin': Localized in Memphis, Tennessee, is hip-hop with a Southern feel. Originally a very punctuated walking style, similar to a "gangsta walk"; later added gliding steps and—pointe work (even by guys)!

Battling: Dancers in a circle, take turns competing against each other with their best moves. Originally created to channel the negative energy of rival gangs into something positive; now blended into the hip-hop technique.

Dance Hall: Hip-hop with a Jamaican feel, is looser and more grounded.

OBSERVE: A HIP-HOP CLASS IN LOS ANGELES

Kenya Clay is a compact firecracker of a dancer teaching at Millennium Dance Complex. The music is loud and pulsating, seemingly determined to alter your heartbeat to its meter. Listen to her instruction—you can feel the passion and almost hear the music.

Don't give away your start. And five, six, and seven! Strong! OOOOOM! Tick, right, left. And *rond de jambe*. Elbow is leading. Give something in the hand. It breathes! Going on my toes (she rises on pointe in her tennis shoes). Da! Da! Da! And Fred Astaire! This is uncomfortably long. And strong! It reads in the line. Energy! Give me a pretty *coupé*. Here comes the groove! From here on out, we are groovin'. Head and shoulders and use that plié. Plié is your friend in hip-hop! And kick, ball, change! [12]

Like ballet and contemporary dance, these separate techniques are becoming more and more blended. This leads to the overall uniqueness of the hip-hop style, juxtaposing short, strong, punctuated movements with extended, flowing, expansive gestures. Hip-hop demands strength, stamina, and control, particularly for the more acrobatic moves.

Name: Connor Ryan
Age: 13
Job (when not studying!): Dance student
Dream Job: Professional dancer, hip-hop

When did you start dancing and why?

Age seven or eight. I took my first hip-hop class and really enjoyed it. I tried lots of sports—soccer, basketball. I didn't really enjoy any of them. I really like hip-hop music; I love the beat. A friend told me about 24/7 Dance Studio [in Maryland], and I tried it out. I thought it was cool, and I wanted to do a cool style of dance.

Why did you decide to enter the Monsters of Hip-Hop competition?

It is one of the best conventions you can go to. You take class with different choreographers, learn a routine, and perform it for the choreographer. It's really, really fun. Then, on Sunday morning, you audition with three hundred kids. Then the judges ask some people to come back and do it again. One of the awards was the overall scholarship to Millennium [Dance Complex]. I also took second place in the Freestyle Battle and won a hundred dollars.

How do you feel about hip-hop?

There are so many different styles. Everybody puts their own spin on the moves. Hip-hop is isolation. You might do a *piqué* or *battement*, but then you do a wave down the body. You have to use all your body. My teacher said ballet would benefit my hip-hop. I also took jazz and contemporary to keep the technique going. I take ballet to perfect the technique.

How do you fit school into all of this?

I have the opportunity to take dance class in high school. We have a really good dance teacher. But I have too many requisites in my freshman year, so I will have to wait to join the dance team in my sophomore year.

What are your plans after high school?

I really do want to get a degree; I'm going to need it. I'd like to have a double major—dance and something else to fall back on. I really am interested in the history of the ancient world, Greece and Rome. It has always been my dream to come and dance in L.A. There are so many different choreographers here. They live here because the celebrities they work for live here. You also get choreographers from Vegas who come here. There are more auditions here and more opportunities. I want to move to L.A. and start my career here, and try and land some gigs.

Get There from Here

Be Smart with Your Schooling

Mix it up; every teacher has a different spin on style. As you become more proficient, start looking up different studios specializing in hip-hop, research their faculty to get an idea of their backgrounds, and watch their class videos online. The bigger studios catering to professionals will have open classes taught by choreographers currently working in this part of the industry. Also, they will frequently have master classes with top choreographers who are staging shows all over the world. This will definitely up your game. If you want to dance, work with the pros; you've got to have the professional edge when you audition as well as when you perform. These studios will also offer summer intensive programs and work in cooperation with various conventions to offer scholarships to their schools.

Put Your Skills on the Line

If you are leaning toward a commercial career, find a competition studio that teaches that type of dance and attends those types of conventions and competitions: ShowStopper, Move, Hollywood Connection, International Dance Challenge, Teen Dance Groove, LA Dance Magic—the list goes on. *Dance Teacher* magazine publishes both a competition guide and a convention guide every year. These supplements will introduce you to the wide variety of opportunities available. The studio where you are studying will send their select students to these gatherings, and you will have the opportunity to take master classes with top professionals, as well as compete against your peers. You should take this opportunity to get accustomed to competing, as you will be doing just that all of your dancing career. As veteran convention judge Cris Judd puts it, "There is always someone better than you at these events. If you think you know it all, you don't. There is always someone to learn from. We're all in this together."[13]

As you move up the competition ladder, you will need to take professional-level classes with professional dancers. Look for studios in your area, like Millennium Dance Center and EDGE Performing Arts Center, both in Los Angeles. These studios are where it's happening, and working alongside professionals who do this for a living is how you up your game. Take the master classes with the people who actually choreograph and tour with the big conventions and work competitions as judges. While New York City is often regarded as the dance capital of the United States, if you find you have more of a commercial bent, you will more than likely want to launch your career in Los Angeles.

 SPOTLIGHT

tWitch:
Ambassador of Hip-Hop

Stephen "tWitch" Boss's breakout performance on *So You Think You Can Dance* first brought him to national attention. He made it to the finals and placed second overall, and he has frequently returned to the show as an All-Star. He was partnered with Kherington Payne on the show, where they danced under the name of "Twitchington" and were extremely popular with audiences. He also partnered with Katee Shean and danced the now legendary hip-hop number "Outta Your Mind" with ballet dancer Alex Wong. In recent years, tWitch has appeared as a guest on the daytime talk show *Ellen*. He even tours the country giving master classes and teaches at South County Dance Company in Rancho Santa Margarita, California.

Talk to People

The bottom line for working in the commercial world is networking—who you know. You will meet people at class; and once you start working, you will meet more people with whom you will want to keep in contact. The job grapevine is always active. With smartphones, text messaging, Facebook, and Twitter, it all turns pretty fast, and you want to be sure you are in the loop.

Be Yourself—Inside and Out

There is no specific body type in hip-hop. It includes all heights, sizes, and ages, ranging from five to seventy. Anything goes. It could easily be said that the diversification of body types and ages is at the core of hip-hop; having emerged from the street, hip-hop must accommodate everyone on the street.

Hip-hop has created its own fashion. Think back to the garb worn by the French at the early stage of dance, in which the dancers appeared in the latest fashions of the day. Hip-hop dancers perform in the latest *street* fashions of the day. Hip-hop as a fashion statement and an art form has crossed social and racial boundaries, allowing it to spread globally.

Know the Money

Most of the work done in music videos is non-union. The average shoot is one or two days. Average pay is $500 to $800 per day. Concert tours are also working nonunion, with an average pay scale of $1,500 to $2,000 per week.[14]

MATCHING
Can You Match the Ballet Scores with Their Composers?

Music is essential to ballet. Not only does it underscore the dramatic beats of the ballet, it supports the dancer with tempo, tone, and quality, whether melodious or strident. You will want to familiarize yourself with the scores of the great ballets, as you will be dancing them over the course of your career. (Everybody does *The Nutcracker* at some point.) Listen intently to the orchestrations; they provide the depth and expression to the musical phrase. Music is the soul of dance. It is what inspires the dancer and elevates the choreography from mere technique to art form.

Can you match the ballet scores with their composers? (Hint: "The Big Three" were all written by the same composer. Another composer listed wrote three of the other ballets.) Happy listening!

1. Igor Stravinsky

2. Claude Debussy

3. Leo Delibes

4. Nikolai Andreyevich Rimsky-Korsakov

5. Leon Fyodorovich Minkus

6. Pyotr Ilyich Tchaikovsky

7. Sergei Prokofiev

8. Adolphe Adam

9. Frédéric Chopin

Coppélia

Swan Lake

The Sleeping Beauty

Peter and the Wolf

Romeo and Juliet

Giselle

Afternoon of a Faun

The Firebird

The Rite of Spring

Don Quixote

Scheherazade

The Nutcracker

Petrouchka

Les Sylphides

ADOLPHE ADAM—GISELLE; FRÉDÉRIC CHOPIN—LES SYLPHIDES; CLAUDE DEBUSSY—AFTERNOON OF THE FAUN; LEO DELIBES—COPPÉLIA; LEON FYODOROVICH MINKUS—DON QUIXOTE; NIKOLAI ANDREYEVICH RIMSKY KORSAKOV—SCHEHERAZADE; SERGEI PROKOFIEV—PETER AND THE WOLF, ROMEO AND JULIET; IGOR STRAVINSKY—THE FIREBIRD, PETROUCHKA, THE RITE OF SPRING; PYOTR ILYICH TCHAIKOVSKY—THE NUTCRACKER, THE SLEEPING BEAUTY, SWAN LAKE

83

Name: Galit Friedlander
Job: Dancer

When did you start dancing and why?
I started ballet at six but quit when my teacher left. Then when I was thirteen, it totally popped into my head, *Why am I not dancing?* I started taking class again—ballet, Hispanic hip-hop, and tap. I wanted to get better, so I took more classes. I was a troubled teenager; I had a lot of dark spots. When I danced, I was in a different world. I would forget the emotional problems. It was very therapeutic. It started developing me as a person. It's not too late to start in middle school. Dance came at the perfect time.

What was your first big decision?
After graduating from the Fiorello H. LaGuardia High School of Music & Art and Performing Arts in New York City, I was accepted to [the] University of Southern California in Los Angeles, the most difficult and amazing choice I have made. USC did not offer a dance major at that time, so I chose theater and communications for majors.

What's next?
I see myself being a choreographer and [a] director. I want to produce art. I am happy to be a consultant on any show that has dance. You have to put yourself out there. You have to be driven. You have to be tenacious. You have to knock on every door. I've built relationships with people. I'm using my communications degree.

5

Behind the Scenes

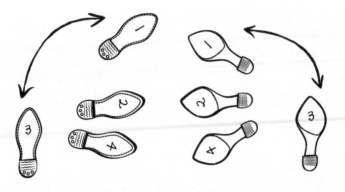

Whether backstage at a Broadway play or behind the camera of a movie, TV show, or commercial, there is a whole other performance going on behind the scenes. Though not seen by the audience, this show is just as synchronized, just as detailed, just as choreographed as the dancing the audience does see. From the stage managers to the crew chiefs to the wardrobe supervisor to those in charge of hair and makeup, all of these individuals must coordinate their departments into a perfectly timed performance. In many ways this backstage ballet is even more complex and fascinating to watch than what is onstage! If the show behind the show isn't tight, the show onstage is headed for a train wreck. It is these individuals working behind the scenes who ensure that the show does indeed go on.

WHAT'S IN YOUR DANCE BAG?

You can always spot a dancer by the dance bags they carry over their shoulder as they walk down the street or ride buses and subways. The dance bag is indispensable, as it carries each dancer's individual needs for class, rehearsal, and performance. These are some of the items you will find in a dance bag. What will you put in yours?

★ Ace bandage

★ Ballet slippers

★ Barrettes

★ Bobby pins

★ Cell phone

★ Character shoes

★ Cologne

★ Hairbrush

★ Hair elastics

★ Jazz Oxfords

★ Leotard

★ Pen and notepad

★ Pointe shoes

★ Scissors

★ Shrug

★ Small LED flashlight

★ Socks

- ★ Surgical tape
- ★ Sweatshirt
- ★ Tights
- ★ Toe protectors
- ★ Towel
- ★ Trail mix
- ★ Water bottle

With all that is stuffed into a dance bag, you would think it belonged to either Mary Poppins or Hermione Granger!

All the Moving Pieces

From the Top

It starts with the producer of a Broadway show or the artistic director of a dance or ballet company. The producer can be one individual or several, or a producing entity such as the Shubert Organization or the Nederlander Organization. These people decide what show, concert series, or ballet they will produce in a given show or performance season. Once that decision is made, the producer is responsible for everything necessary to get the show on the road and ensure there is audience to watch it. A producer's responsibilities include:

- ★ Securing the funding to produce the show

- ★ Arranging for rehearsal space

- ★ Booking a theater and/or tour

★ Hiring production staff, which includes the stage managers, publicist, and of course, any stars appearing in the production

The producer also finds and hires creative staff, such as the composer, the orchestrator, the book writer, and the lyricist, as well as that all-important visionary: the director/choreographer, who is responsible for "turning straw into gold"—making something out of nothing and turning it into a hit.

Five, Six, Seven, Eight!

The director/choreographer has creative control of the show. It is this person's vision that comes to life on the stage. The director/choreographer works with the producer to hire the appropriate staff—costume designer, lighting designer, set designer, musical director/conductor. All of these individuals must coordinate their efforts with the director/choreographer for approval of the smallest detail that goes on the stage.

Name: Freddie Peterson
Age: 19
Job (when not studying!): Dance student
Dream Job: Dancing with Sitra Dell or Kyle Abraham

When did you start dancing and why?

I started dancing when I was little; I came from a troubled home. I was raised by a single mother. She was the head of the dance ministry at our church, and dance was an outlet. I started training when I was fifteen. A lot of what I had learned was wrong. I had to start over. I didn't know a piqué turn! I worked so hard. I moved the table in the living room to dance.

Why did you audition for the 2013 American Dance Festival?

I improved so much that my teacher, Lisa Wilder, told me I had to go elsewhere to grow. She told me to audition for the American Dance Festival. [Peterson danced a site-specific work choreographed by Mark Dendy. A group of eighty dancers gave two outdoor performances at Lincoln Center in the summer of 2013. Using the existing terrain, the dancers were asked to dance in the water, on stairs and railings, roll on the ground, and work with the pillars of the Metropolitan Opera House.]

How do you feel about contemporary dance?

I wasn't sure if I wanted to go into contemporary and concert dance. We take a ballet class every day—a lot of ballet and stretches. In the dance ministry, we encourage the congregation to offer [themselves] to God. People are really touched and engaged by the choreography.

How do you fit school into all of this?

I met Brenda Daniels [assistant dean of dance at the University of North Carolina School of the Arts] at the American Dance Festival. She encouraged me to audition for the UNCSA high school. I left public high school to do my senior year at UNCSA. My senior year of high school was equal to my freshman year of college.

What are your plans after graduation?

It would be awesome to have a job in a dance company when I graduate. My best friend graduated and lives in New York, so I plan to room with him. Before, I was scared of the world, scared of rejection. I am ready now.

What about your social life?

It was really hard because I was new to the [high school] senior class. [Now] I have some great friendships. I had to double up on my classes so I could graduate with my class.

●●●●●●●●●●●●●●●●●●●●●●●●●●●

Do, Re, Mi

You can't dance without the music, so the composer is brought in to write the score for a Broadway show, new concert piece, or ballet. Older, established pieces already have a score—like *The Nutcracker* or Alvin Ailey's *Revelations*—but new works require new music; and that is the job of the composer. In a Broadway musical, the show really revolves around the score. Once the music is written for any production, it is arranged by an orchestrator, who takes the composer's melodies and expands them to be played by the various musicians in the orchestra or pit. The fully orchestrated score is then handed over to the musical director/conductor.

Downbeat

The musical director/conductor is in charge of hiring the musicians, rehearsing them, and coordinating the music with the director/choreographer tempo (how fast or slow the music is played), dramatic timing (as in when the music starts and stops), and how loudly the music is played. In a Broadway show, the musical director is also in charge of all the singing for both the leads and the chorus.

La, La, La

Of course, in order to sing a song there has to be words, which are written by the lyricist. Composers and lyricists work as a team. Some famous match-ups include composer Elton John and lyricist Tim Rice (*Aida*) or composer Alan Menken and lyricist Howard

Ashman (*Beauty and the Beast* and *The Little Mermaid*). Each team works according to what suits them best. Sometimes, the lyricist will write the words first then hand them to the composer to write the music. Other teams work the opposite way, with the music being written first and the lyricist setting the words to the existing music. Some work together composing both words and music, side by side. And sometimes, one person is capable of writing both the words *and* the music, such as Phil Collins (*Tarzan*) or the brilliant Stephen Sondheim (*Merrily We Roll Along*). In a Broadway musical, the songs and dances are designed to extend and continue the dramatic beats and the storyline, and someone has to write that story. Enter the book writer.

MUSIC MATTERS

Pyotr Ilyich Tchaikovsky, the first classical composer to take the writing of a ballet score seriously, composed the score for each of the "Big Three" ballets: *The Sleeping Beauty*, *Swan Lake*, and *The Nutcracker*. As Tchaikovsky's dance expert, Marius Petipa went so far as to specify exactly how many measures, or bars, he wanted in each section of music, solo variation, and *pas de deux*. The partnership proved to be magical—one that opened the door of Russian dance to the Western world.

Line!

The book writer is in charge of telling the story and giving the actors the words or lines to speak. (Some book writers also write lyrics). The book writer crafts the story that will be told onstage using only dialogue. Some scripts have stage directions, others don't. (Some directors pay attention to the writer's stage directions, others don't.) The book threads everything together. While some concert-dance pieces and ballets do not have story lines, the big-story ballets, such as *The Sleeping Beauty* or *Swan Lake*, all have written scenarios that break up the action into acts.

Painting the Picture

The set designer's job is to create the settings in which the story of the show takes place. This could be anything from a quaint French country town (opening of *Beauty and the Beast*) to a sumptuous castle ballroom (*Swan Lake*, Act III) to a sparse African savannah (*The Lion King*). Sets make the magic happen, as they provide the background, the framework, and the look of the show. Of course, when it comes to working with dancers, the set designer must be sure that the sets don't get in the way of the dancers while they are performing. For this reason, all the set designer's plans must be approved by the director/choreographer before construction begins, which is why three-dimensional scale models of the sets are built to demonstrate not only what they will look like but how they will change fluidly from one scene to the next.

SERIOUS BUGS

Just like new technology often has bugs today, the new theater technology in 1600s France—*les merveilleux*, "the marvelous ones"—frequently malfunctioned. This left the levitating god or goddess stranded midair and then yanked ungracefully upward; or worse, propelled dangerously downward. Not so *merveilleux*.

What Am I Wearing?

Now that the dancers have a setting in which to work, they have to be dressed according to the time period of the show. From fantastic fairy-tale costumes (*Sleeping Beauty, Beauty and the Beast*) to basic leotards and tights (*A Chorus Line, Concerto Barocco*), all cast members must be correctly attired. This is the job of the costume designer. Designing wardrobe for dancers presents different challenges than designing for actors who don't have to move in the same way. Costumes must not be constricting, fabrics must give; and they also have to stand up to being worn many, many times (a Broadway show does eight performances a week). Costumes bring the characters to life, and all the costume designer's sketches must be approved by the director/choreographer before they are made.

Lights Up!

Now that there are sets and costumes, the lighting designer breathes life into them with lighting. The lights create the mood of each scene, changing according to the dramatic content of the action. A bad light design can destroy the best sets and costumes while a good one compliments and brings out a three-dimensional quality, making everything look believable. The lighting designer creates a light plot that determines which lighting instruments will be used, exactly where in the grid they will be hung, and how they are to be focused. Lighting designers also use different colored gels placed in frames over the lighting instruments so they can have a palette of colors to work with—just like an artist painting on an easel. All of the lighting designer's work must meet the approval of the director/choreographer.

Places, Please; House Out; Stand by Curtain

Coordinating all of these disciplines is the job of the production stage manager (PSM). This person is the captain of the ship, telling the crew what to do and when to do it. With a big show or ballet, the PSM has assistants (ASMs) to help keep things running smoothly. The PSM is brought on board early-on during preproduction. The PSM:

★ Arranges for a space to hold auditions

★ Schedules auditions and publicizes them

★ Schedules meetings for the production staff

★ Coordinates the rehearsal schedule according to the director/choreographer's needs

★ Sets calls for the dance rehearsals at specific times

★ Schedules wardrobe fittings

★ Schedules technical rehearsals

★ Runs the show once it opens

★ Schedules understudy rehearsals and "put-in" rehearsals for new company members

★ Deals with any and all problems backstage and onstage

The PSM will "call the show" during rehearsals, previews, and for a time, after it has opened. Once the show has settled, one of the assistants is delegated to call the cues.

The stage manager calls the show from a headset that is connected to the crew members so they can be in constant communication during a performance. In a large production, cameras and television monitors are positioned at specific points both onstage and backstage so the stage manager can see what is happening at all locations throughout the performance. The stage manager calls the show from a show bible. This is the lifeblood of the show; it's how the magic happens. Developed (and changed many times) during rehearsals and previews, the show bible consists of the script and every lighting cue, music cue, special-effects cue, sound cue—absolutely everything that happens both backstage and onstage—in sequential order to ensure a smoothly running performance. Each cue is assigned a number and a letter that the stage manager calls out over the headset at specific points in the script. Then the various crews respond.

You will find it interesting that the stage managers and the crew belong to two different unions: stage managers are members of the Actors' Equity Association (AEA) while all crew members belong to the International Association of Theatrical Stage Employees (IATSE). The lines of responsibility are clearly drawn by the unions and there can be no crossing over. While the stage manager governs what is happening on the stage, he or she is not allowed to hang or focus lighting instruments, move scenery or props, or assist with wardrobe. Those are the jobs of the appropriate crew chiefs and supervisors.

 SPOTLIGHT

Marty Kudelka:
The Core Is the Key

Commercial choreographer Marty Kudelka travels the country and the world, holding master classes in hip-hop and choreographing for such celebrities as Justin Timberlake. He often works with Monsters of Hip-Hop, Millennium Dance Complex (Los Angeles), and the Alvin Ailey American Dance Theater company in New York. "You need to have a solid technical foundation," said Kudelka in an interview with *Dance Teacher* magazine. "You need to know where your center is and understand how to move strongly from your core."[1]

Spread the Word

Publicity and marketing are essential to any dance company or Broadway show. Stage productions must compete with television and movies, school activities, the internet, and video games, as well as other dance companies. With all that competition for an audience, publicity and marketing are key to filling the seats in the house.

Publicity and marketing do the following:

★ Identify the target market for the company or show and decide how best to advertise to that audience

★ Solicit, arrange, and organize media interviews (print, radio, television, and online)

★ Design and place ads

★ Arrange for publicity stunts to attract attention to the show or dance company

★ Maintain the company's website and social media

★ Organize promotional events and conferences

★ Coordinate handling of critics, including contacting them, securing complimentary tickets for them, and compiling press packets for them

★ Oversee the archiving of all press clippings, video clips, photos, and online links

All these people in these positions are necessary to have a well-run production.

But, if you want to be performing that production how do you get onstage? Enter the agent.

Show Me the Money!

While professional actors and athletes have long had representation, that was not the case in the dance world, particularly in Los Angeles, where you had to know someone to hear about an audition and then obtain an invitation to attend. This is no longer the case. Now, professional dancers are represented by talent agents who keep track of auditions and schedule appointment times for their clients to be seen. No more cattle calls!

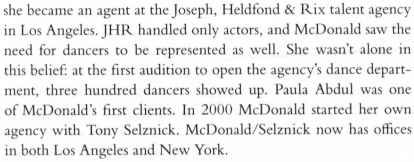

It will come as no surprise that it took a dancer to recognize, understand, and address this need. In the 1980s Julie McDonald was a professional dancer who also owned a dance studio in Venice, California. When she was sidelined by an injury, she became an agent at the Joseph, Heldfond & Rix talent agency in Los Angeles. JHR handled only actors, and McDonald saw the need for dancers to be represented as well. She wasn't alone in this belief: at the first audition to open the agency's dance department, three hundred dancers showed up. Paula Abdul was one of McDonald's first clients. In 2000 McDonald started her own agency with Tony Selznick. McDonald/Selznick now has offices in both Los Angeles and New York.

As a dance agent, you arrange for auditions for your clients and handle the negotiations when a client is "booked," or hired, for a job. For your services, you take a 10 percent commission from each dancer's paycheck. You are not allowed to be paid up front; your clients have to be working in order for you to get paid. Your 10 percent comes out of the fee that is negotiated *above* the dancer's minimum payment (or scale) as required by the performing unions. For example, you will frequently hear a contract negotiated for scale plus ten.[2] If you are an agent in Los Angeles, you will help your clients find work largely in television, film, and commercials. On rare occasions, you may handle negotiations for a stage production, but there is very little theater produced in LA. In New York

City, you will help dancers find work on camera as well, but a larger share of the work will come from booking theater gigs. For the dancer, it's ideal if your agency is bicoastal, with offices in both New York and LA. But maintaining two offices at either end of the country is twice the work, requiring twice the staff and twice the expense. More than likely, your agent will have established an association with another agency in the city opposite your home base. After all, agents want their talent working in as many different performing venues as possible. Why be limited to stage or screen? An agent wants their clients' names in lights everywhere!

Name: Kent Zimmerman
Job: Actor, singer, dancer, choreographer, director, paralegal, massage therapist, event coordinator, administrative assistant, receptionist—or more simply put, jack-of-all-trades

Why and how did you take up all these careers?
The arts have always been a part of my life, my blood. My grandparents introduced me to theater at a very young age, and something about it stuck. It wasn't until I was in high school that I actually had the opportunity to participate in community theater, and that's when it became serious. Everything else I do, outside the theater, I do out of the necessity to live. Pay bills. Buy groceries. Have a bit of fun.

What type of education did you pursue to enter these careers?
I graduated from the University of Cincinnati, College-Conservatory of Music, majoring in musical theater. It is a four-year conservatory that gave me a bachelor of fine arts. But the best education I have gotten over the years has been

just doing. Auditioning. Rehearsing. Listening. Performing. I enter every situation as a learning opportunity, because we are ever growing.

Who helped you further your career in this field?

My mentors: Larry Evans, who was my first director in community theater in high school. Joel Ferrell, who I have assisted over the years. Without their trust and willingness to give me the opportunity to try, I wouldn't be where I am today. My teachers: Aubrey Berg, the head of the musical theater department, and Diane Lala, my first dance teacher, from the University of Cincinnati.

What type of work and/or volunteer experiences helped you gain the contacts you need to achieve your career goals?

I try to say yes to as much as I can, even if I'm not entirely sure I know how I will complete the given task. Jump and the net will appear below you.

What is the most difficult part of your job?

The rejection. Trusting that you are exactly where you need to be to be available for whatever may be around the corner.

What is the most rewarding part of your job?

Walking out onstage after a performance or wrapping up a day at the studio or the office and knowing that I did the best I could; and with the gifts that I was given, touched someone. Affected someone in a way that they needed that very moment.

What advice would you give to kids interested in this work?

Follow your dreams. No matter what they are, no matter how difficult you may think it will be. If something inspires you to try, don't stop. Never give up believing. Never give up on yourself.

When you were a kid, did you think you would enter this profession?

No. Growing up, I wanted to be a teacher. And looking where I am today, I realized that is exactly what I am doing: teaching through my passion.

From Onstage to Backstage

Then there are the backstage careers that make abundant sense for the transitioning dancer to pursue: wardrobe supervisor, in charge of keeping all costumes organized and in good shape; wig supervisor, in charge of all hair pieces worn by the cast, including mustaches and beards (and some pretty wild dos if you are doing *Lion King* or *Cats*!); and dance captain, in charge of the dancers and keeping the show clean. If you have been paying attention to what has surrounded you in rehearsals and performances (as you should have), you should have a good grasp on what it takes to get the show on the road.

Name: Polly Baird
Job: Dancer and dance captain

When did you start dancing and why?

I started dancing when I was three or four at Stanley Holden's [ballet school] in Los Angeles. We moved to New York when I was eight, and my mother took me to audition for the School of American Ballet. She didn't tell me I was auditioning; I thought they just put numbers on me. I started in the first division at eight and stayed through eighteen.

What was your first big decision?
My mom suggested I audition for *The Phantom of the Opera*. At that point, I was at my ballet pinnacle. I wanted to be in ABT. I turned up my nose at *Phantom*, but I went to the audition anyway. After the dance audition, I wanted to leave. I packed up my stuff. They kept eight of us to sing. I had great trepidation about this; I did everything wrong. I hadn't seen the show. I walked in wearing shorts and flip-flops. I didn't know where to stand or where to look.

What's next?
We have a kind of joke backstage: what's your plan B? Whatever I do, I would need an undergraduate degree. I have been working with medical therapy dogs, using them in my father's pediatric practice at Columbia University. Having an outside interest helps to keep your sanity.

As dance captain for *The Phantom of the Opera*, Baird is responsible for every movement on the stage. She works with stage management, calling and conducting "cleanup" rehearsals, understudy rehearsals, and put-in rehearsals. "I sit on the other side of the table now. I see the other aspects of the business. You start looking at things like directing or stage management."

It's All On Your Head
Nathaniel Hathaway had talent as a dancer. He was awarded scholarships to the University of North Carolina School of the Arts, Pacific Northwest Ballet, and Central Pennsylvania Youth Ballet and was a member of the Dance Theatre of Harlem ensemble. But despite all that, he realized he was never going to be a soloist. He started customizing pointe shoes for Capezio and also found work as a dresser. Eventually, he began substituting as a supervisor backstage on Broadway shows.

"I have the ability to take command," he said in an interview with *Dance Teacher* magazine. "which I think is natural for ballet dancers and important as a supervisor."[3]

The connections he made led him to getting his own job, ultimately, as a wig supervisor. "You are the go-between for the wig designer, director, and stars. You mesh all the information from these sources plus your research to make the right look happen. I think that ability to tinker until it's right is a dancer's perspective."[4]

6

Teamwork

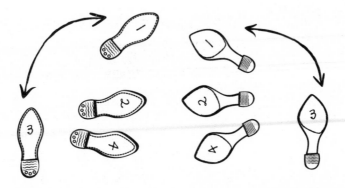

It is an invaluable part of your career and education as a dancer to have a good support team and know how each member of your team can help keep you tuned up for top performance.

Medical personnel are some of these people. Often for a dancer, in the case of injury, the frustration factor overrides the pain factor. There are times when you can work through an injury and times when you should not. More often than not, recognizing the symptoms and treating them immediately will prevent more serious injury later. Pushing yourself—and your injury—too far will only cause further damage, and delay your healing and return to performance.

Allynne Noelle, principal ballerina of the Los Angeles Ballet, snapped a ligament in her right foot earlier in her career. She continued to dance on it for ten months. She was accepted to the National Ballet of Canada but could only stay with the company for three months, as her foot was causing her too much difficulty. She had to return home to have surgery. Recovery was very difficult for her. She was on crutches for six weeks and became depressed. Fortunately, the surgery was successful (they replaced the ligament with an artificial one), and she is now dancing again. "I was twenty-two, stubborn, and stupid,"[1] she admits, and she knows she should have taken care of the injury immediately.

 # SPOTLIGHT

Ray Mercer:
A King of the Broadway Jungle

Ray Mercer has been in the cast of *The Lion King* for over eleven years. He was first a part of the national touring company for two years, and then he joined the Broadway cast. "This is not a show you can phone in," he said in an interview with *Dance Magazine*. "You need to be prepared every time, without fail. No excuses."[2]

Mercer first trained as a gymnast. When he took his first ballet class at seventeen, he changed course. He worked very hard to develop his technique, and his extreme discipline carries over to his brutal eight-performances-a-week schedule.

Mercer's preshow warm-up consists of a hundred push-ups, work at the ballet barre, and special attention paid to his achilles tendons, as he does many jumps and handsprings in the show. Then he stretches. *The Lion King* is an unusual show in that it is not only very athletic, the costumes of the actor/dancers are actually large puppets, which means they have extra weight to carry. (Mercer is a giraffe on stilts.) Mercer counteracts this by working out in the gym four times a week, in addition to taking class to keep his technique in form. During the performance itself, Mercer will do more push-ups backstage to keep his energy up—a total of five hundred per show.

"Get all the training you can," he advises. "You must have a firm work ethic; without it you'll never survive."[3]

AVOIDING THE PITFALLS OF STRETCHING

As a professional dancer, you have to be at the ready at any time. Rehearsals, in particular, will not provide a warm-up; you are responsible for that yourself. This is also true of some classes. So many injuries can be prevented if you take the time to stretch before and after dancing. Here are new, safer ways of accomplishing two traditional stretches.

Quadriceps stretch for the front of the thigh: You probably grab your foot behind your body, arch your back, and push the foot toward your buttocks. This puts stress on your lower back, the weakest area of the spine. Try kneeling on the floor about eighteen inches away from a wall instead. Extend one leg back, bending at the knee, and place the instep of that foot against the wall. (Your weight is being held by the supporting foot on the floor and the thigh.) Gently push back to stretch the quadriceps. Change legs.

The straddle stretch: This is generally done by sitting down on the floor with your legs in as wide a second position (straddle) as possible. Then you walk your hands out until your torso is flat on the floor. However, this runs the danger of the hips rotating in, overstretching the ligaments of the hips. The better way to straddle stretch is to sit with your legs wide, body erect, and hands behind your legs on the floor. You can do *port de bras* from side to side to increase the stretch. According to Dr. Kristian Berg, a specialist in the treatment of sports and dance injuries, the purpose of stretching (other than it feels good) is to achieve "maximum stretch with minimal joint movement."[4]

In the Wings profile

Name: Will Repede
Age: 10
Job (when not studying!): Dance student
Dream Job: Professional dancer

When did you start dancing, what style do you dance, and why?

I started dancing when I was in second grade. I dance all different types of dancing, but my favorite is hip-hop because it was the first class I did. I also do ballet. I decided to try it because my teacher Daniel did ballet, and it made him better at all his other classes. Last year I started jazz because my teacher Wendy suggested it. I got to skip a level because I started late, and Wendy thought I should. I think that if I hadn't done ballet I wouldn't have skipped a level.

Why did you decide to audition for the competition team?

I decided to audition for competition because it looked like fun and it would be the first traveling team I had ever been on. I wanted to be on a traveling team because I enjoy staying at hotels. Another reason I wanted to be on the competition team is because I have a friend who is on the team and is my age, so I could be in some of the same classes as her.

How do you feel about dancing in competition?
I think it is fun and makes great conversation with my friends at school. I like it because I like to dance on a stage.

How do you fit school into all of this?
I mostly have dance after school but otherwise on weekends. I have dance on Wednesday for two hours, on Friday for forty-five minutes, and on Saturday for one hour and forty-five minutes.

What do you plan on doing after you graduate from high school?
I plan on getting a bachelor's degree in dance at a school that offers dance as a major. I'm hoping Winona State University [in Minnesota] offers dance as a major. I hope so because that's where my mom went to college.

What about your social life? What do your friends think about your dancing?
At first my friends from school were surprised, but after that they were very interested. I think they were surprised because not very many boys in Rochester, Minnesota, take dance. At my studio there's one boy who's older than me and another who's my age, and a lot of younger boys.

Align Yourself

Dancers swear by their chiropractors. The correct alignment of the body is essential for everyone but even more so for a dancer. Chiropractors work with your body, keeping it healthy when you are in good form and getting you back on your feet quickly when you are injured.

Center Stage *profile*

Name: James Van Grinsven
Job: Doctor of chiropractic medicine

Why did you become a chiropractor?
When I was playing sports in high school, I injured myself, and the chiropractor helped me get back into the game sooner than a medical doctor.

What type of education did you pursue to enter this career?
I have a degree in biology from California State University, Northridge, then four years of chiropractic college at Southern California University of Health Sciences.

Who helped you further your career in this field?
The chiropractor who introduced me to the profession, Joseph Vampa.

What type of work or volunteer experiences helped you gain the contacts you need to achieve your career goals?
Local business chapters such as Business Connections and Business Network International. In addition, I volunteer at Hart Park. [A public park in Santa Clarita, California, named for William S. Hart, the silent film actor who starred in the early westerns of the 1920s.]

What is the most difficult part of your job?
Shifting a patient from the medical paradigm, which is to take medication or surgery, to the chiropractic one of healthy recovery and prevention.

What is the most rewarding part of your job?
When I show a person who was thinking there was no hope to get better how to get better naturally.

Do you find that dancers have a different outlook regarding their bodies and have to adapt your course of treatment for them?
Most dancers already have a good idea about health and how to maintain it. I step in when they lose their health and show them new ways to regain their health through chiropractic.

When you were a kid, did you think you would enter this profession?
I knew I wanted to become a chiropractor at age sixteen, after meeting one who was knowledgeable and helped me get back into sports.

TOP 10 DANCE INJURIES

1. Neck strain is usually caused by choreography that uses excessive head movements, such as head rolls.

2. Pain in shoulders and upper arms results from lifting and catching your partner.

3. Lower back strain is pain in the small of the back (lumbar region) from excessive arching and lifting.

4. Snapping hip syndrome is a weakness in the outside of the hip. The dancer will feel a snapping in the front of the hip joint and hear a sound much like that of a large rubber-band snap.

5. Weakening knee cartilage means it loses its protective shock-absorbing ability due to too much pressure being put on the kneecap.

6. Tears in the knee cartilage happen after an over-rotating turnout; or a twisting of the knees can cause the knee cartilage to tear.

7. Shin splints come from jumping on an unsprung floor (cement!), dropping the medial arch, and excessive ankle rolling. These can all overwork the tibial tendon and cause it to tear.

8. Achilles tendonitis results from the overuse of the Achilles tendon, working on a hard floor, or putting too much pressure on a tight calf muscle.

9. Lateral ankle sprain is a ligament tear occurring when the outside of the ankle joint rotates inward due to loss of balance.

10. Ankle impingement is a pinching sensation at the back of the ankle when pointing or in *relevé en pointe*. Sometimes this impingement is caused by having an extra bone in the foot.

Massage It Out

Working in cooperation with chiropractic medicine are the massage therapists. Nothing feels better on sore or tired muscles than a good massage, and stimulating blood flow can help an injury heal faster.

Name: Natalya Velichko
Job: Massage therapist

Why did you become a massage therapist?

I think I came to it genetically. My dad had amazing healing hands. He had books on his shelf in Russia about massage therapy; that was the foundation. I used to look at the pictures. Then one day I decided to try a professional healing massage. It was amazing! My vision was clearer and my whole body felt rejuvenated, so I wanted to be a massage therapist.

What type of education did you pursue to enter this career?

The massage therapist who gave me my first massage opened a massage therapy school six months later. I went to school full-time to get my education and certification.

Who helped you further your career in this field?

Nobody helped me. I did everything.

What type of work or volunteer experiences helped you gain the contacts you needed to achieve your career goals?

I took a part-time job working with an alternative medicine doctor. We worked with patients who had injuries from skiing or car accidents, elderly patients who had had strokes: everything. After three years there, I went to work at a big spa. I worked there part-time for five years and also did private sessions on my own. Then I was able to open my own private practice.

What is the most difficult part of your job?
Patients who show up late or don't show at all. It doesn't happen often, but when I have another booking after their appointment, it gets difficult. My massages last one and a half to two hours—it's very draining physically. I never rush things. I believe in quality, not quantity.

What is the most rewarding part of your job?
Seeing how people feel after a massage and also over time. Also, I develop a relationship with my patients. As their massage therapist, I become part of their life and health. I also help them emotionally; somebody needs to listen to them. It's all connected, the physical to the emotional. I love helping people physically and emotionally, and enjoy every moment of my work.

Do you find that dancers have a different outlook regarding their bodies and have to alter your course of treatment for them?
Dancers, people who use their muscles, are very strong on the outside but sensitive inside. Dancers are thin and don't have much mass, but their muscles are dense; and I have more work to do, especially with the men. One hour can feel like two. I can go deeper into their muscles, but they are fragile inside. Ballet dancers have very sensitive legs and can't take much pressure there. They can take more pressure on their backs, between the shoulders.

When you were a kid, did you think you would enter this profession?
I think it was always in the back of my mind because of my father. I would see pictures of massage therapy in his books and was curious about it from the time I was about ten. But I wanted to be a model then and did do some modeling when I came to the United States.

FITNESS FOR EVERY BODY: ONE DANCER'S ROUTINE

Julia Burrer arrives at the rehearsal studio forty-five minutes ahead of her call time and begins her own warm-up. "Our rehearsals sometimes start with a full run of a piece, so you have to get your heart rate up and get a little sweaty before-hand," she said. Burrere is a member of the Doug Varone and Dancers contemporary dance company in New York City. At six foot one with a six-foot arm span, she cuts a solid figure onstage.

When Burrer started to feel pain in her lower back, she con-sulted several different doctors and bodywork specialists, each of whom had a different opinion as to what the injury was. Taking a bit of information from each specialist, she combined all the information into a specific routine of exer-cises she uses to warm up, protect, and correct the bulging disc in her back.

Burrer is also very conscientious when it comes to nutrition. Since there is little time for eating in her daily rehearsal sched-ule, which runs from 10:00 AM to 4:00 PM, she comes prepared with high-protein snacks like yogurt, nuts, and fruit. It's light and "you don't feel overfull . . . It's all about balance."[5]

The Better the Fuel, the Better the Performance

You have probably heard the expression, "You are what you eat." As a dancer, you put high demands on your body, and you must fuel it properly to meet those demands.

Name: Brian Gonzales
Job: Health coach

Why did you become a health coach?
Most people start off eating badly and continue to do so; it starts at home with the parents. It has become essential that kids are educated about nutrition outside the home.

What type of education did you pursue to enter this career?
I don't have a degree. I was trained by an Herbalife doctor who specializes in nutrition.

Who helped you further your career in this field?
We build a bond with the other coaches here; we are like a big family. We help each other with personal development and lifestyle change. We are big on mentoring.

What type of work or volunteer experiences helped you gain the contacts you need to achieve your career goal?
We . . . speak at schools, and have Lifestyle Day and weekend boot camps to get people involved in exercising and educated in nutrition. It's nutrition and fun. So much of what we do is giving back to the community. I love to give back.

What is the most difficult part of your job?
Following up with clients to make sure they are staying on their program. It's all in the follow-up.

What is the most rewarding part of your job?
Getting texts from clients who are happy with the nutritional

program I have developed for them. Having made a change in someone's life is really rewarding.

Do you find dancers have a different outlook regarding their bodies and have to alter your course of treatment for them?
I was a search-and-rescue swimmer in the navy, so I understand that kind of athleticism. But I was not in the best of shape when I was doing that. You can't outwork a bad diet. A lot of dancers have a poor diet and think they can do that.

When you were a kid, did you think you would enter this profession?
Absolutely not.

Teach Them Well

And let's not forget the people who got you to this point in your career—the teachers whose dedication and diligence molded you into the dancer you are now.

Sheryl Baxter practically grew up in her mother's dance studio in Wisconsin. She began her training at age eight. In the summers, her mom took her to New York to take class in ballet, tap, and jazz. Sheryl went on to have a successful career dancing in movies, television, and on Broadway; and did national tours of *42nd Street*, *Sophisticated Ladies* (with Gregory Hines), and *Cats*. It was during the tour of *Cats* that she decided it was time to switch gears. Baxter moved to Los Angeles and began teaching tap at the American Musical and Dramatic Academy (AMDA) Los Angeles campus, in addition to such well-known studios in LA as that of Andrei Tremaine and the Roland Dupree Dance Academy. "My passion now is to pass on the steps," she said. "I've been lucky; I've never had another job. A dancer always continues."[6]

Corrinne Glover has been teaching dance since she was a college student. Though she was well-trained in the RAD ballet technique by her mother, Glover had no desire to be a professional dancer and was enrolled at San Francisco State College as a theater major. When Glover was in her junior year, her mother needed another teacher at her dance studio and "commandeered," as Corrinne said, her help. Corrinne has been teaching ever since; is the artistic director of a small ballet company in Santa Clarita, California; and absolutely loves teaching, which is "very rewarding. Some of [my students] have been with me since they were four years old. I have watched them grow up and go on to have careers with Boston Ballet, San Francisco, and the Joffrey."[7]

Erica Sobol's classes in contemporary dance are jam-packed at EDGE Performing Arts Center in Hollywood, California. After class, the line of students waiting to thank her for her work snakes down the hall outside the studio. She remains in the hallway and graciously receives each dancer—upward of forty. Erica continues to travel worldwide, teaching her unique style of grounded and expressive dance. "I am much more about the process than the performance," she said. "I love being in class. If you know where your center is, I can work with you."[8]

IS THERE A DOCTOR IN THE HOUSE?

In addition to successfully staging his own shows, Gower Champion had a second career as a show doctor. Before the days of workshopping a show, a new musical would tour to different cities to work out the bugs before it opened on Broadway. When the show wasn't working and it looked like it was going to turn into one of the biggest Broadway disasters on record, the call went out to Gower Champion. Arriving incognito, the cast unaware of his presence, Champion would watch and study the troubled show. Somehow, word would filter backstage that Champion was in the house, and the cast and crew would heave a sigh of relief: help was on the way. With Champion taking the directorial reins, they just might have their Broadway run. Champion was able to save quite a few shows from becoming flops. In some cases, he even refused to take credit for his work.

AVOIDING THE PITFALLS OF ACCIDENTS AND INJURIES

In any physical endeavor—basketball, football, soccer, or dancing—there are bound to be some mishaps along the way. Injuries and accidents happen; it's an occupational hazard. The severity of the injury is what is important, and there are ways to keep from being sidelined.

Protect yourself by taking care of yourself. Always allow more than enough time to warm up prior to rehearsal or performance. Rehearsal schedules are very tight, and there is no time allotted for an official company warm-up. You are responsible for yourself. Get to rehearsal early (your stage managers will already be there), and make sure you are physically and mentally prepared to work the moment the choreographer walks through the door.

Use quiet times well. During rehearsal, you will find that there is a substantial amount of time when you will not be dancing; the choreographer is thinking things through, changing his or her work, or simply working on a section of the piece where you are not involved. Be respectful; be quiet; and keep your muscles warm by wearing leg warmers and sweatshirts, and gently continuing to stretch your muscles when they are not being used. Trying to dance when you have been standing or sitting still for thirty minutes or more is asking for trouble.

Be diligent. When it's showtime, get to the theater early and allow adequate time to prepare yourself for each and every performance. This is where the majority of dancers fall out. Once you have an established performance schedule, it is easy to start taking short-cuts. Don't. You must remain disciplined. Have a set performance drill and always follow it. You must also continue to take class every day (yes, even when you are on tour—*especially* when you are on tour); it's part of the job. You will lose your edge technically and mentally if you are not in class every day. Even though you are dancing every night, the choreography in the show will not work all of your muscles, and you will be out of shape. You may find that you are the only one doing a full barre before the second show; that's okay. Stay focused on your performance. You can only be responsible for you, and you must always deliver the best you can.

7

Art about Art

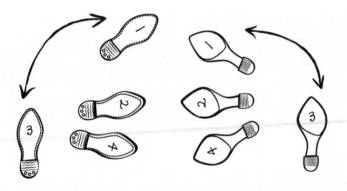

All of the following avenues and more are open to you if you have an interest in dance but don't want to pursue it onstage. If you are considering college, you might want to think about a double major—dance along with journalism, creative writing, or photography. Or you could pursue a dance major with an interest in choreography and directing. You will find all these occupations require an understanding of rhythm, tempo and tempi changes, key changes, orchestration, and expression.

Step It Out

It was Balanchine who insisted that the credit for his work in *On Your Toes* read as "choreography by . . ." rather than "dances by . . ." It was the first time this credit was given for a Broadway show, moving the choreographer out of the wings and into the spotlight.

Today, the captain of the ship is the director/choreographer, and no one reaches that status without having been a dancer first. Ballet really came of age when the French dancer Marius Petipa took the artistic and choreographic reins of the Russian Imperial Ballet. Balanchine was trained at that same Imperial Ballet School and then turned the art form inside out by inventing neoclassic choreography for New York City Ballet and Broadway. Joffrey trained with Mary Ann Wells in Seattle before taking on the two big companies in New York, training dancers and then choreographing works to achieve his goal of having his own company. Graham learned her technique from Denishawn, then founded the first dance company in the United States and created her own works. Taylor danced with Graham and then emerged to stage his own work for his company.

THE BIRTH OF A CHRISTMAS CLASSIC

Balanchine was not interested in "story ballets," so it is truly ironic that he is responsible for introducing *The Nutcracker* to this country. Frequently considered an American tradition, this ballet was unknown in the United States until Balanchine staged it in 1954 as a tribute to the Christmases he experienced as a child in Russia: the magnificent decorations, the heightened sense of expectancy, and everyone dressed in their best as they waited in suspense for the magical moment. Balanchine himself actually played the toymaker Drosselmeyer in a 1958 telecast of the NYCB production.

Training and dancing with the Paul Taylor Dance Company, Twyla Tharp later became one of the most inventive choreographers of the twentieth and twenty-first centuries. Jerome Robbins was a ballet dancer with New York City Ballet and American Ballet Theatre before he choreographed *Fancy Free* for ABT and

West Side Story on Broadway. Gower Champion, prominent in the MGM musicals as a dance team with his wife, Marge, also choreographed big production numbers for the movies before he staged blockbuster Broadway shows like *Hello, Dolly!*. Fosse also danced in Metro Goldwyn Mayer movie musicals before making his stylistic mark on Broadway with *Pippin* and *Chicago*. As a teenager, Michael Bennett toured in an international production of *West Side Story* and danced on the TV show *Hullabaloo* before he entered Broadway legend as the director/choreographer of the revolutionary show *A Chorus Line*. These are the choreographic greats, and they were all dancers first.

Center Stage *profile*

Name: Sha Newman
Job: Choreographer

When did you start choreographing?
When I was sixteen. I thought I was going to assist the choreographer, but then was told I was doing the whole show.

What prompted your decision to switch from dance to choreography?
After a ten-month bus-and-truck tour of *Annie*, I had had enough. I decided to make the transition to start staging shows rather than dancing in them. At first, I assisted other director/choreographers, I then worked strictly as a choreographer before I decided to assume the responsibility of the entire production. You have greater control over the entire project. But not every dancer can be a choreographer, and not every choreographer can be a director. A director has to see the whole picture. I have always seen the whole picture like a big movie; the dance has to continue the story. It's not about the steps.

What's next?

I haven't done Broadway yet, but I sure would like to.

DANCING THROUGH THE MOVIES

1. *Top Hat* (1935)
2. *Swing Time* (1936)
3. *Shall We Dance* (1937)
4. *The Red Shoes* (1948)
5. *An American in Paris* (1951)
6. *West Side Story* (1961)
7. *That's Entertainment!* (1974)
8. *That's Entertainment, Part II* (1976)
9. *Roseland* (1977)
10. *The Turning Point* (1977)
11. *Fame* (1980, 2009)
12. *Breakin'* (1984)
13. *Footloose* (1984, 2011)
14. *White Nights* (1985)
15. *Dancers* (1987)
16. *Dirty Dancing* (1987)
17. *Tap* (1989)
18. *Strictly Ballroom* (1992)
19. *That's Entertainment! III* (1994)
20. *Flamenco* (1995)
21. *Lord of the Dance* (1995)
22. *Riverdance* (1995)
23. *Dance with Me* (1998)
24. *Dancemaker* (1998)
25. *Tango* (1998)
26. *Billy Elliot* (2000)
27. *Center Stage* (2000)
28. *Save the Last Dance* (2001)
29. *Honey* (2003)
30. *Broadway: The American Musical* (2004)
31. *Shall We Dance?* (2004)
32. *You Got Served* (2004)
33. *Ballets Russes* (2005)
34. *Mad Hot Ballroom* (2005)
35. *Roll Bounce* (2005)
36. *Step Up* (2006)
37. *Take the Lead* (2006)
38. *The Kirov Ballet: Swan Lake* (2006)
39. *Hairspray* (2007)
40. *How She Move* (2007)
41. *Planet B-Boy* (2007)
42. *Stomp the Yard* (2007)
43. *The Royal Ballet: The Sleeping Beauty* (2007)
44. *Every Little Step* (2008)
45. *Mao's Last Dancer* (2009)
46. *The Nutcracker* (2009)
47. *Tutu Much* (2010)
48. *First Position* (2011)
49. *Joffrey: Mavericks of American Dance* (2012)
50. *The Royal Ballet: Romeo and Juliet* (2012)

Center Stage *profile*

Name: Erica Sobol
Job: Choreographer

When did you start choreographing?
I have been creating dances since I was a little girl. When I was in high school, instead of PE, I had the chance to take modern dance. It was a lot fun. We did a lot of choreography. With all my heart, I wanted to be a choreographer.

What prompted your decision to switch from dance to choreography?
I was a theater major for three years, but it just wasn't working. The dean of the dance department agreed to structure a personalized theater/dance major for me. I was way, way behind. I was nineteen when I took my first dance class, and twenty-one when I took my first ballet class! I didn't start my professional dance training until I started taking class at Broadway Dance Center in New York. I worked with hip-hop teacher/ choreographers Kevin Maher and Rhapsody James there. Hip-hop really influenced my musicality. It is a departure from the through-line of music that everybody does. I learned to really listen to the music, to the orchestration—the vibration so quiet you might miss it, a drum in the background. Very little sounds the same on second hearing. It's a playground in there!

What's next?
My work is a mixture of contemporary fused with hip-hop. I am continually trying to blur the line between theater and dance.

No Filter

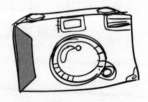

In the dance world, being a photographer can be a difficult job. Your subject, the dancer, is constantly in motion. So often, the shot reveals the preparation for a step rather than the spectacular result.

Angela Sterling was a dancer with Pacific Northwest Ballet when she had a conversation with ballet photographer Steven Caras that got her thinking. Caras told her the only people who should take pictures of dancers are dancers. Later, after a severe spinal injury, she decided she wanted to try photography. She took a course in still photography, then spent eight months in Europe taking pictures for ballet companies in Amsterdam, Munich, Dresden, and Monte Carlo. She is now the exclusive photographer for Pacific Northwest Ballet. "I know instinctively when to shoot; the clients don't have to go through the images. I give them three hundred perfect position shots they can use."[1]

SPOTLIGHT

Pina Bausch: Unique, Controversial

Although the innovators of modern dance were mostly Americans, their work was first recognized, lauded, and adapted—by Europeans. Pina Bausch was one such European. Bausch first studied dance with Kurt Jooss in Germany; then, at age eighteen, she won a three-year scholarship to the Juilliard School in New York. She took what she learned there from Antony Tudor and José Limón and developed her own, very unique, highly controversial work.

Returning to Germany, she worked as the artistic director of the Wuppertal Opera Ballet. One year later, she veered away from the traditional, founding her own company in 1973. Bausch began to experiment with choreography, using both voice and theatrical gestures in her pieces. At first, her work seemed improvisational, but the choreography was solidly rooted in classical technique and very challenging for the dancer. Bausch took her inspiration from life, observing many different types of people. Her stark and sometimes brutal dance dramas were highly criticized and rejected; people walked out of her concerts. But later pieces focused on exploring the lighter side of humanity.

Send It to Press

With the interest in dance being so widespread now, there are many magazines and books dedicated to the subject, not to mention newspaper articles, backstage interviews, and critical reviews. Somebody has to write the copy. It is amazing how many dancers become writers. Flip through a *Dance Magazine*, *Dance Spirit*, *Pointe* or *Dance Teacher* and look at the bottom of the article, where you will see a brief description of that writer's background. Here are a few examples:

Kathleen McGuire regularly writes for *Dance Teacher*. Her bio after many of her articles reads: "Kathleen McGuire is a former dancer. She also writes for *Dance Magazine* and *Pointe*."

Jennifer Homans, a former professional ballerina, wrote *Apollo's Angels*, an extraordinarily comprehensive account of the history of ballet that was named one of the best books of the year by the *New York Times Book Review. Entertainment Weekly* praised her work, stating that she brought ". . . a dancer's grace and sure-footed agility to the page."[2]

Lauren Kay writes for *Dance Magazine*. Her bio? "Lauren Kay is a dancer and writer in NYC."

Name: Alexis Johnson
Age: 20
Job (when not studying!): University student
Dream Job: Dancer, a contemporary ballet company

When did you start dancing and why?
I was six. Since I loved ballet, I took class three or four times a week with a very strict teacher.

Why did you audition for UNCSA (University of North Carolina School of the Arts)?
In the ballet world, most dancers go straight into companies. I had had only one ballet teacher at that point; I didn't feel like I was ready. I needed more training. I auditioned for three colleges. I loved the audition for UNCSA. I visited [the campus], and it felt right. UNCSA has the best ballet program. I loved how serious the teachers were about it. [It was] the training I needed. I decided to give it one year at UNCSA . . . and am now going for my BFA (bachelor of fine arts).

How do you feel about contemporary dance?
The teachers are so supportive. I had never done a contemporary program, so I wanted to try. They pushed me in a way I had not danced before. I've never been so sore!

What are you plans after college?
I took a summer intensive at ABT. The teachers at the JKO School—they were amazing. But I'm [now] more of a contemporary dancer, and ABT is so classical. I don't have my heart set on ABT; I'm keeping my options open. In the dance world, if you don't keep your options open, you won't be a success.

THE COPASETICS

The Copasetics was a group founded in 1949 by twenty-one African American men who had danced on vaudeville stages and wanted to preserve tap dancing. They met once a week at a member's house or at the Showman's Café in Harlem, told fond stories of the old days, and danced. These men both preserved and explored different rhythms, expanding the art of tap dancing for generations to come.

Critics

Dance critics attend dance concerts, ballets, and Broadway shows and evaluate the dancers—both corps and soloists, as well as the productions as a whole. Sarah Kaufman, dance critic for *The Washington Post*, was awarded the Pulitzer Prize for her "refreshingly imaginative approach to dance criticism."[3] Before becoming a dance critic, Kaufman studied dance, but she noted, "I always knew I was cut out for writing, more than dancing."[4] She earned a degree in English from the University of Maryland, then went on to do graduate work in journalism at the Medill School of Journalism at Northwestern University. She began her writing career by freelancing for *The Washington Post* and being mentored by Alan M. Kriegsman, the first journalist to win a Pulitzer Prize for his work in dance commentary. Kaufman took his position when he retired.

Alistair Macauley is the chief dance critic for the *New York Times* and the former chief theater critic for London's *Financial Times*. His review of New York City Ballet's *The Nutcracker* earned criticism for the critic because he referred to principal ballerina Jennifer Ringer as having "eaten one sugar plum too many."[5]

What preparations does he take before reviewing a company? "My job is to review performance," he said. "I find I avoid people who tell me what they think tonight's is going to be like . . . I like to be quiet in my seat for a few minutes beforehand. The more relaxed I am, the better . . . It's wonderful to know that, having seen *Swan Lake* three hundred times, I can be moved again by a striking new performance."[6]

AVOIDING THE PITFALLS OF DRUGS

Gelsey Kirkland was a phenomenally talented ballet dancer in the School of American Ballet. At fifteen, George Balanchine invited her to join the New York City Ballet, making her the youngest member in that company's history. She was only seventeen when Balanchine staged a new production of *The Firebird*, featuring her in the title role. In 1974, Kirkland became a principal with ABT and fell into drug abuse. She began skipping company class and showed up late to rehearsals—if she showed up at all. Temperamental and demanding, she became so unreliable it was a constant guessing game as to whether she would actually dance any of her scheduled performances. In her book, *Dancing on My Grave*, Kirkland admits, "I became so injury prone and undependable, bets were placed at the front of the theater on whether I would perform."[7] She was fired by ABT.

Dancing on My Grave is Kirkland's own story of her descent into drugs and her arduous climb out. It is a must-read for anyone considering a career in any field of dance. Dance is a consuming career, and in an effort to stay on their feet, there are those who will rely on substances to meet the demands of a rehearsal/performance schedule or to decompress after a performance. This is not a good idea. No matter how many of your fellow dancers are using drugs, no matter what the peer pressure, you do not want to fall into that trap. Understand this now: you are not invincible, impervious, or immortal.

When he was dancing in New York, Alex Castillo had a friend who was a medical student working in a hospital emergency room. Drug use among the ballet companies in New York was so common that whenever a dancer was brought to the ER, the staff immediately assumed it was due to an overdose of cocaine. As a dancer you must have your body in top form in order to earn a living. Drug abuse, cigarettes, and alcohol abuse will not only destroy your body, they will also give you the reputation of being unreliable and destroy your career. More than other professions, this is a social industry. You may feel pressured to do what everyone else is doing for fear of being outcast. Decide now, well in advance of ever facing the situation—and you *will* have to face this situation—exactly how you will handle it. It is much easier to decline if you have already rehearsed the scenario in your mind. You already know how important rehearsals are, so play out this scene to ensure a successful conclusion.

WORD SEARCH
Broadway Musical Word Search

Can you find six or more movies that went on to became a musical on Broadway? (There are fifteen in total.) Be sure to look in all directions.

```
E N S H R E K T H E M U S I C A L U
T T V F R F J N G J F I Z P T E T K
H G S B X H O V E A R G P H Y S L T
E G G I P T H T L W P Z E N A T J H
L L Y H N Y U A E N S R I E L O L E
I L D Y D G D P J N E I B J K O F L
O B E J L D I J A D M E E W F B V I
N H B G I P B N S D H T T S K Y L T
K O R N A D E H I T X A E E D K X T
I R B P O L O N D N E X B L N L L
N E X L A E L N O Z T B W L N I A E
G P T L S D A Y A T H H U D D K H M
I T H W T Y W N B W I Z E G I G I E
K M H C T J F W C L R G K R V K O R
M M D U M I G K Y D O K N I A N J M
W O A E E F Q X D L V N A I C I G A
Y E U A W S C C I T D K D E R N N I
B T O I L L E Y L L I B Q E A B K D
```

8

Life with a Side of Dance

{by Kristin Thiel}

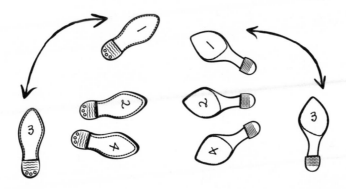

Not everyone will grow up to have a job in dance—and that's okay! One of the best things about dance is that you can participate in it even if you work or study in a different field. Dance is an awesome part of life.

Center Stage *profile*

Name: Lindsay Putnam
Day Job: Biomechanical engineer
Dance You're Studying: Latin styles, primarily salsa

Did you dance as a kid? What style?

I did ballet as a little girl but stopped when I was ten or eleven. In college I picked up swing—East Coast and Lindy Hop—and did it socially and a couple of times competitively. I also took a few ballroom lessons, which I liked but didn't have the money or time to do it semipro.

Why did you decide to pick up dance (again) as an adult?

I found myself looking for ways to get out of my normal social scene and remembered loving swing dancing in college. I couldn't find much in Portland [Oregon] in the way of swing dancing, but I saw a huge salsa scene. I just picked a dance on a night I had free and went for the lesson, then dancing. [Since then] I haven't missed more than two or three days of salsa dancing in a row, even when traveling!

What's the hardest thing about dancing as an adult?

Learning to let loose and be silly. When you're trying new things or getting creative in styling, footwork, or shines (solo dancing while your partner dances independently), sometimes you feel foolish and self-conscious. Even in a really familiar crowd, it can feel like you're telling a story, and halfway through you lose your train of thought and start rambling; and everyone thinks you're ridiculous. It takes some practice to realize that the people who notice are noticing because they have fun watching *you* have fun . . . and everyone else is paying attention to their own dancing. So you can do what you want!

What benefits have you seen?

I'm generally an outdoor enthusiast, so historically I gain weight and stay in a lot in winter. With dancing, I'm never bored or feel like I haven't gotten exercise. Even with my outdoor activities, when I started dancing, I lost thirty pounds. My social network is much wider, my confidence has improved greatly, and I'm just generally happier. With dancing several nights a week and performances every few weeks, I always have something to look forward to. I also love being the center of attention, and dancing is a good way to do that in a socially acceptable manner.

What are your dancing plans?
My contract just ended with Son Latino Dance Company, and my partner and I have decided to go our separate ways while he focuses on things other than dance. I will find a new partner and start a new choreography with two other members of Son Latino for performance. And I have just found a partner with whom I intend to compete On-2, which is a different style of salsa, in June. I'd also like to dedicate a little time to improving my other dances. Tango, kizomba, and ballroom can all have great styling impact in salsa, so learning them would only improve my Latin dance. Someday I would really love to open a studio for dance, though they're in no short supply in Portland. I also intend to spread the love as much as possible and bring people out dancing every chance I get.

Dance Like Nobody's Watching— Even When They Are!

Would you smile and laugh and feel good if you remembered, throughout your life, to dance as much as possible? You don't need to follow a routine or remember any specific steps; there doesn't even have to be any music playing. Feel the rhythm of your body as you slide and jive almost every moment of the day.

★ Dance while you brush your teeth

★ Dance while you make your lunch (just put down the knife first)

★ Dance while you take your dog for a walk (Or see if your cat or guinea pig may want to go for a twirl. You can even dance in motions that imitate your fish!)

★ Dance on your way to class or as a warm-up before any other physical activity you might be doing (Remember Olympic athlete Kate Hansen who warmed up by dancing to Beyoncé songs before she competed in the luge?)

PUT YOUR MONEY WHERE YOUR FEET DANCE

Jerome Robbins established the Jerome Robbins Foundation in 1958 to support dance, theater, and related arts. His organization also dedicated resources to fighting AIDS when the disease first appeared in the early 1980s.

Someone Is Dancing Somewhere

There are so many ways you can take up dancing as a hobby or pastime activity. Every night of the week, people go out dancing. Often, for very little money—and sometimes for free—you can join them.

In the Club

Dance clubs are one popular option, and some are even all-ages, with venues open to teenagers. Check out what's happening in your area and talk to your parents—you may be able to dance at one of these clubs soon. Here, people gather with their friends to eat, drink, and most importantly, dance. This is not a formal dance event; it's a casual and fun way to hang out. But you may see some real moves on the dance floor! Keep your eye out for budding stars, and show off some of your style too. Sometimes there's even a dance contest. Why not look for those and join in the fun? You may even win a prize.

Clubs usually feature a DJ, but sometimes there is a live band. Either way, there will be some great music—pop, electronica, Latin, fusion, or something else entirely. Clubs either specialize in a type of music or have a calendar that rotates through different options.

There may be a cover charge, which means you pay money to get in the door, and there also may be a dress code. Some places let you come as you are, but some want you to put on your twirlingest dress or flashiest shoes.

Center Stage *profile*

Name: Rebecca Pillsbury
Day Job: Writer
Dance You're Studying: Lindy Hop and blues

Did you dance as a kid? What style?

Though I always wanted to dance as a kid, I didn't enroll in dance classes until I was in college! My university offered a swing and social dance class that introduced me to traditional ballroom styles like the waltz, fox trot, tango, and swing. I fell in love with swing and later discovered a variation of swing dancing called Lindy Hop, which led me to my favorite style— blues dancing.

Why did you decide to pick dance up (again) as an adult?

I wanted to express my spirit with my body in a way that was physically challenging, creative, and fun! I found dancing to also be a great way to meet people and travel. Many cities around the world host what are called "lindy exchanges" and "blues exchanges," where dancers from different states and countries come together to learn about emerging dance styles and techniques. Therefore, it's easy to connect with locals and gain insider knowledge of almost anywhere you travel to!

What's the hardest thing about dancing as an adult?

Physically keeping up with younger, more agile dance partners! Lindy-Hop dancing, especially, can be quite physically demanding, so you need to be in good shape. Age alone, however, should never be a deterrent for any style of dance—I see plenty of people well into their seventies dancing Lindy Hop with great ease and style!

What benefits have you seen?

Dancing has benefited me mentally, physically, and spiritually, in so many ways. Mentally, it has helped me get over my fears of meeting new people and going to parties where I don't know anyone. It has helped me stay in good athletic shape and to become comfortable using my body to fully express who I am. It has also given me an appreciation for all different styles of music, and offered me an outlet for expressing the pure state of unbridled joy.

What are your dancing plans?

I plan to keep on dancing until the day I die! I cannot imagine my life without this beautiful form of self-expression. I am also planning to write a book about the power that dancing has to transform lives.

DANCING ALONG THE GREAT WALL

Members of the Atlanta Hawks Cheerleaders and Harry the Hawk, the basketball team's mascot, have cheered their team on in China during three-on-three tournaments for several years. It's awesome when you have the opportunity to travel while doing what you love!

Learning Your Lessons

In many cities, you can take a dance lesson every night of the week and then show off what you've learned by staying for the music. These events aren't just held at clubs or bars but at dance studios, cultural and community centers, and cafés. Some may not allow young people, so call first to see if there are any age restrictions. Then show up without reservations, pay a small entry fee, and learn a dance as taught by an expert dance teacher. It may be swing, ballroom, salsa, or something you've never heard of before! Bring a friend or two if you want, but you don't have to. Usually during the lesson, the teacher asks students to switch partners anyway. When you're dancing in real life, you won't always be able to dance with the same person, so learn how to have fun with lots of people.

The lesson usually lasts about an hour, then it's time for even *more* fun! The band or DJ starts in earnest. More experienced dancers arrive to join in, and it becomes a regular dance party. You may have just learned lots of new steps, but don't worry about remembering everything. You're there to have fun, and you'll probably remember more steps than you realize. Just listen to the music and watch others. Ask one of your fellow students or the teacher (who usually stays to dance too) to dance. Even the people who didn't come to the lesson usually love to help beginners. Remember, the best way to up your game is to work with someone more experienced than you. You did come here to learn those particular steps, after all!

Name: Marilyn Chow
Age: 12
Job (when not studying!): Student
Dream Job: I want to be very talented in ballet and very passionate about it, but I have other talents and don't want my job to be ballet. I don't have a dream job in mind yet, but I've thought about being a children's speech therapist. I also love dogs and would like to work with them. I do want to stay involved in ballet, though.

When did you start dancing and why?
I started dancing when I was two and a half years old. I started dancing because I enjoyed music and loved to move.

Why did you decide to audition for the Oregon Ballet Theatre's Keller production of _Dream_ (Christopher Stowell's _A Midsummer Night's Dream_, based on the classic Shakespearean comedy)?
I actually didn't audition for this production. Instead, the children's rehearsal director came in to observe our normal ballet class and choose who would be in the production. I was very happy when I found out I had been chosen.

How do you feel about dancing in such a major production?
I felt really happy and very inspired by the all of professional dancers and the way they express emotions to tell a story

through dance. It made me want to dance more and participate in many other productions. It was a great opportunity to work with and learn from the professional dancers. It was also a great chance to perform in front of an audience after all the hard practice—especially since there are not many performances that involve my level.

How do you fit school into all of this?
Most of the time I had to do all of my homework a day or [two] ahead of time because there wasn't enough time to do it on rehearsal days. I would have to keep on top of new homework assignments and stay very motivated and focused to get the work done; I couldn't waste any time. I would also have to remind my teachers [of] the days that I would be absent or leaving early. I had to say no to sleepovers and parties until the production was over.

What do you plan on doing after you graduate from high school?
After I graduate from high school, I want to go to a good college, but I want to keep up with ballet. I want to keep my talent, passion, and enthusiasm.

What about your social life? What do your friends think about your dancing?
I have many friends who are really impressed but aren't into dancing, and many friends who used to dance when they were little. Some of my friends still dance, and we love to talk about what we're doing in ballet. All of them have different interests, but all support my dancing and understand when I say I can't go to their birthday party or sleepover because I have ballet.

Celebrate Good Times

There are so many festivals and other celebrations throughout the year. Some are cultural, some are religious, and some are for a whole neighborhood or city. Dance is often a component of these events. Community groups may perform a dance that fits the type of celebration, or there may be an open dance just to have fun. Definitely attend those open, informal dances. Why not? But you may also want to consider joining a more organized group to learn what type of dance will be done and practice beforehand.

These groups rehearse throughout the year and may require their dancers to wear costumes or some type of coordinating outfit. Check what the commitment is for each group and if there are any age restrictions. The good thing is that these groups are made up of a variety of people, young and old, who work or study different things at different times. This means that the group is often very accommodating to its members' busy lives. This type of dancing is a fun hobby that fits in with all the rest that you do.

 SPOTLIGHT

Georgina Pazcoguin: Success Through Patience and Perseverance

They say all good things come to those who wait. A talented dancer, Georgina Pazcoguin was accepted to NYCB's corps when she was eighteen. She began her ballet studies at age four under the guidance of the Allegheny Ballet Company then progressed to the demanding Pennsylvania Youth Ballet. She spent three summers and one winter at the School of America Ballet on a scholarship before being offered an apprenticeship to the company. Pazocoguin was offered a position in the corps after finishing high school at the

Professional Children's School. She didn't quite fit the standards of a Balanchine ballerina; "they didn't quite know where I was going to fit in,"[1] she said. But her talent was more than evident, and she excelled in the Jerome Robbins works like *Fancy Free* and *NY Export: Opus Jazz*. She also stole the show dancing Anita in *West Side Story Suite*, a collection of dances from the musical, choreographed by Jerome Robbins. Her press notices were outstanding, but still her rank in the company was *corps de ballet*.

Frustrated but already having one toe in the water of Broadway musical theater, Pazcoguin decided to explore this medium further. She took a two-week workshop, where she found herself among Broadway dancers and singers. She was also offered the opportunity to work with the newly formed chamber ballet company Ballet Next. In the off season from City Ballet, she was able to dance with Ballet Next and more fully explore her talent.

Finally, after ten years in the corps, Pazcoguin was promoted to soloist. "I have a feeling of . . . an immense sense of relief," Pazcoguin said in an interview with *Dance Magazine*. "This is my home, and I hope it will stay that way."[2] Patience and perseverance pay off.

Part-Time Performer

If you have more time and skill to commit to dancing but you still don't want to be a pro, you may look into part-time dance work. One option is dancing for a sports team. Sports dance squads entertain the crowd at all home games and perform at community, charity, corporate, and promotional events. They all are required to have a full-time job or be a student with part-time employment. While being on a dance squad is considered a hobby, that doesn't mean it's easy to do. A dancer who proves she has the ability and personality to dance on the team must attend *all* events and rehearsals. You simply can't hold a rehearsal without all the dancers there.

CLOGGING AS DANCE THERAPY

In 2007, nearly five hundred teenagers gathered at The Hague in the Netherlands to attempt to beat the Guinness World Record for the most clog dancers dancing at the same time. The cloggers danced the Dutch clog dance from the ballet *La Fille Mal Gardée*, choreographed (and originally danced) by Stanley Holden for Britain's Royal Ballet. While clogging is not usually found in traditional dance venues, Danny Daniels choreographed "Clog and Grog" for the Broadway musical *Walking Happy*. Clogging was also used in the finale of the Broadway version of *Seven Brides for Seven Brothers*. And now a very creative thirteen-year-old has developed an unusual and unique use for her clogging skills: therapeutic clogging to help mentally and physically disabled persons.

Caitlin Jalinsky has been clogging since she was four years old. She has also done gymnastics and some tap and ballet, but she kept returning to clogging. She has performed at some of the big clogging competitions in Utah, Arizona, and Las Vegas. She also came very close to getting a slot on *America's Got Talent*.

In the summer of 2013, however, matters took a different spin. Caitlin spent a week at a summer camp in Big Bear City, in the San Bernardino Mountains of California. During that week, her group had the opportunity to spend a day with a camp for disabled persons. That interaction gave her an idea: what about a week-long clogging camp for the physically disabled and mentally challenged?

Caitlin created her own program and put it on paper. "My mom has friends who work for the Easter Seals Camp in Big Bear City. She submitted it to them, and I was invited to be a camp kid."

The age range of the disabled campers is from sixteen to seventy. Some learn an actual clogging routine; and for those in wheelchairs, Caitlin created "hand clogs" so that those campers could do the clogging patterns and rhythms with their hands instead of their feet. "You don't have to stand up to dance," Caitlin said. "[The campers] stay for an hour and are having a lot of fun. They never thought they could do anything like this."

On the last night of the camp, all 115 campers came together for a talent show. "Some of the campers danced with me—a simple routine," Caitlin said. Those who had been taught to clog with their hands performed their work. "I can't believe I'm doing this!" was a frequent comment from Caitlin's cloggers.

Caitlin plans to further develop her program and expand it for 2014. "I saw mentally and physically challenged people, and I wanted to give back. They are always so much fun to be with. So I thought we could combine dance with them and have even more fun. I have to make some adjustments [for next year]. I want to create a dance just for them."

Center Stage profile

Name: Emily Han
Day Job: Book acquisitions editor
Dance You're Studying: I'm currently learning ballet for adults.

Did you dance as a kid? What style?

I learned some tap as a kid; and then in high school, did some modern dance/jazz.

Why did you decide to pick dance up (again) as an adult?

I love and have a deep appreciation for dance and dancers. It's something I wish I had seriously learned as an adolescent, and now I'm making my wish come true as an adult. I guess it's never too late.

As a child, I remember my love for dance musicals and movies with Gene Kelly or Fred Astaire. In my teens, I had a passion for Bob Fosse and his choreography, and [for] modern dance. The physicality and artistry of the body in motion is such an amazing and disciplined creative form.

What's the hardest thing about dancing as an adult?

Well, your body isn't as flexible and strong [as it was when you were] younger. Luckily, I do a lot of yoga and stretching, so that helps. But your body does need more time to rest and heal from the aches.

What benefits have you seen?

I feel my muscles are more toned, and I have much better posture. You get in touch with your body in a way that brings awareness and coordination—better focus and concentration as well.

What are your dancing plans?

I'm going to keep learning as long as I can and my body lets me—I love it! It brings me a lot of joy, and keeps me feeling fit and young while being creative!

9

To Degree or Not to Degree—
That Is the Question

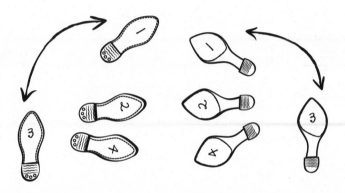

Once upon a time, not so very long ago, the thought of a dancer going to college was, well, unthinkable. The conventional wisdom was (and sometimes still is) since the shelf life of a dancer's career is so short, you needed to join the professional ranks—if you hadn't done so already—directly upon graduating from high school. There was no time to waste. If you spent four years pursuing a higher education, the theory was that you would be horribly behind those who had already jumped onto the stage of the big leagues.

Times have changed. Dancers take better care of themselves now and their careers last longer. There is also more information available as to how to avoid and rehabilitate an injury. There has been a major shift toward professionalism on college campuses, and they have become your best springboard into the "real world" of the performing dancer. College has become the future of the dance industry.

THE FIRST AFRICAN-AMERICAN BALLERINAS

Janet Collins was the first African American dancer to join the Metropolitan Opera Company.

Delores Brown was one of six black dancers accepted to the School of American Ballet. She joined the first all-black ballet company, the New York Negro Ballet, in 1957 and toured England, Scotland, and Wales.

Raven Wilkinson toured the United States with the Ballet Russes of Monte Carlo until the troupe hit the Southern states in the 1960s, where the situation became very dangerous for her. She left the country and pursued her dancing career in Holland as a soloist with the Dutch National Ballet.

School Dances

In recent years, college programs have developed ongoing working relationships with many contemporary companies. Schools often invite these dancers as guest teachers and artists in residence. You will get a good idea as to each company's choreographic orientation and technique this way, and it's a great way to make connections. By working with some of the staff and company members, you will gain a reasonably good understanding of how that company functions and whether or not it is one you would like to pursue.

And what about ballet? Can you get the correct training and exposure to the right people at a college or university? Aren't those four years between ages eighteen and twenty-two even more important to someone who wants a ballet career? Shouldn't you be apprenticed to a company or in the corps by the time you are seventeen? Isn't twenty-two too old to enter a ballet company?

This tried-and-true train of thought might not be taking all things into consideration for today's dancer. As with most decisions, there are pluses and minuses on both sides of the equation.

First, the idea of college for dancers is not as new as you might think. Ruth St. Denis founded one of the first college dance departments in the United States at Adelphi University in 1938. Clearly, it has taken some time for the idea to catch on, but now there are an astonishing number of colleges, universities, and conservatories that offer excellent training taught by superb teachers with real-world experience. These programs can provide the much-needed bridge to a thriving career. Students can expand and improve their training while simultaneously testing the waters of the professional world and acquiring a higher education. (You do need to think about your second career.)

Name: Barry Finkel
Job: Director of education at the American Musical and Dramatic Academy (AMDA), Los Angeles

What do you offer your students?

We offer our students the ability to transfer to the other [New York] campus. Halfway through their curriculum [in LA], they are given the option to apply to the [New York] campus [and vice versa]. [For example], students working for their certificate in dance can spend one year at one campus and the second year at the other campus. The four-year bachelor of fine arts program [BFA] is available only at the Los Angeles campus, as there are certain classes only offered here that they must take in order to get the degree. However, they can transfer to the New York campus for one semester at the beginning of their third semester.

Do you advise your students to sample both cities, as their career will undoubtedly have them traveling back and forth on a regular basis?

Between New York and LA, the industry isn't that different. It's the culture of each coast that is different.

AMDA is a conservatory school, fully accredited by the National Accredited Schools of Theatre (or NAST), correct?

Yes. All the students are here for performance. All our training is conservatory-style training taught by teachers still active in the industry. The entire student body is devoted to the performing arts. AMDA offers four different eight-semester programs leading to a BFA in acting, musical theater, dance, and performance art. We have students who graduate and go on to schools like Yale for their masters. AMDA auditions and accepts applications across the United States and internationally. The school admissions policy is somewhat different from other colleges in that it is not limited as to how many students it will accept. Fall is our largest enrollment, with 700–750 students [on the LA campus]. We have a very thorough adjudication process. Each student is evaluated individually. If we feel a student is qualified for our programs, we accept them. It makes scheduling a nightmare, but it makes the school great. Our goal is to train the most diverse dancer.

The American Musical and Dramatic Academy offers two-year certificate programs in acting, musical theater, and contemporary dance. However, if a certificate student at either campus changes course and decides he or she would like to pursue a BFA, the credits accumulated in the certificate program will be applied toward the BFA degree. The option of transferring campuses still applies.

If you are interested in a career in New York as a dancer on Broadway or with a contemporary dance company, you can spend a significant amount of time continuing to work on your degree while you get the feel of living and auditioning in New York. This way you don't have to go into the city "cold," trying to figure out the subway system, find a place to live, and get a job all at the same time. New York is a very different, highly stimulating, exciting, and heavily populated place to live. AMDA's exchange program offers you a dress rehearsal of what your life will be like in either the Big Apple or LA.

Far from operating in academic isolation, colleges and universities now offer dance programs of such quality that their artistic profiles have become attractive to major dance companies seeking new recruits. College has almost become a necessity in the world of contemporary concert dance. The connections that students make via the guest teachers brought in by their respective colleges is an outstanding "who's who" in contemporary dance.

A good example is the University of North Carolina School of the Arts in Winston-Salem. Brenda Daniels, assistant dean and professor of dance, described the mission statement of UNCSA as: "To train a really strong technical dancer who could go into diversified dance."[1] The university's goal is to have students who graduate and go on to dance on Broadway, or with ballet or contemporary companies.

Name: Brenda Daniels
Job: Assistant dean and professor of dance at the University of North Carolina School of the Arts

What do you offer your students?

We have a strong liberal-arts core. The dance majors take classes in acting and singing, a well as [in] science, anatomy, kinesiology, and nutrition. It's about balance. As the students work through the curriculum, part of the program includes producing their own show. The Pluck Project, so called because "it's very plucky that we're doing this," requires that students start from scratch; . . . do their own fundraising and publicity; [and] generate their own mailing lists, costumes, and staging—everything that needs to be done to get a show up and running.

How have college-level dance programs changed?
There has been a real shift in ballet; there are more applications to join college ballet programs and more students staying for the full four years. Ballet companies want older dancers who are more cognizant as to their bodies, and they have less substance abuse issues.

"Every four years, UNCSA produces a full-scale musical using the original choreography whenever possible," Daniels continued. "For example, when they did *West Side Story*, they performed the Jerome Robbins work; and for *Oklahoma!* they revived the Agnes de Mille material from the 1940s."[2]

UNCSA encourages its faculty to continue being active in the professional world while teaching. The school is also tapped in to such dance luminaries as Twyla Tharp, who chose twelve students from the program to create a dance for the Kennedy Center Honors. *Sweetfield* was done as a tribute to the first woman astronaut, Sally Ride, and the UNCSA students performed the piece at the Kennedy Center in Washington, DC. The second company of Hubbard Street Dance Chicago has been in residence at UNCSA both performing and teaching.

And what about a ballet major in college? Just how viable is that, and why would a ballet dancer go to college in the first place? You will want to investigate different colleges and what they offer as it pertains to ballet. The University of Utah has a connection to Ballet West. Indiana University's Jacobs School of

Music has a terrific ballet program, as does University of North Carolina School of the Arts.

Name: Joe Blocker
Age: 21
Job (when not studying!): University student
Dream Job: Dancer, American Ballet Theatre

When did you start dancing and why?

My father was a professional dancer with Houston Ballet in Texas and put me in ballet class as a child. But my brother told me it was stupid, so I quit. My dad played drums to accompany West African dance classes and I picked up that skill. I started playing the classes. After high school, I got a job playing for a college graduate class. I was around dance so much, I thought I should try again. My dad is fifty-seven and can still do the splits, so I figured I would take a class to be more flexible. I just wanted to be able to touch my toes. My dad thought I would enjoy ballet more, and I was "recruited" by Greensboro Ballet.

Why did you audition for UNCSA?

I met Warring Conover, a teacher at UNCSA, who suggested I look into the university's ballet program. I thought at twenty-one I was too old to go some places, but it seemed like a pretty prestigious and unique place.

How do you feel about contemporary dance?

Contemporary is new, but it's not unfamiliar. I've seen it for so many years. The hardest part is letting my spine go. I have really enjoyed the technique part of it.

What about your social life? How do your friends feel about your ballet career?

I'm trying to get my friends interested. They don't understand what guys do in dance. They think I have to dance on pointe and ask [if it hurts] my feet. I tell them [that] I don't put my feet in those shoes. My friends are excited and proud of me when they see me dance.

What are your plans after college?

UNCSA has a very strong connection with ABT. You can audition here for every major company around the country. I'll see what they think as to how I am progressing. If they think I'm ready to audition, I will.

●●●●●●●●●●●●●●●●●●●●●●●●●

Across the country, in Valencia, California, is the California Institute of the Arts. The school was founded by the late Walt Disney and is a conservatory for dance, music, acting, animation, and visual arts. The idea was for all the arts to be integrated, so all five departments are housed under one roof in one (very large) building in an effort to foster interaction and collaboration among the students in all the art forms.

The premise of CalArts is a bit different from other arts conservatories, as it is not strictly focused on performance. Recognizing that not all dance students are interested in performing, or that they may want to diverge into a related discipline later in their careers, the CalArts dance department offers programs not only in choreography but also in theater craft and technology.

Name: Laura Berg
Age: 21
Job (when not studying!): College student
Dream Job: Dancing with a traveling company

When did you start dancing and why?

I started dancing at age four. I didn't get serious about it until I was twelve or thirteen; that's the age of decision. Most people become self-conscious and quit. I was focused on ballet because my studio, LA Ballet Academy, was focused on ballet.

Why did you decide to audition for CalArts?

CalArts is very open; they are not trying to encourage "cookie cutter" dancers. Dancers are encouraged to be unique. I also did not want to be in LA. It's more commercialized, with the hip-hop influence and lots of tricks. This was my first choice.

How do you feel about the program here?

I like doing things that are different to me. There is something more intelligent in contemporary. [In] ballet, you have to internalize the steps to make them fresh. Contemporary changes every day. You need to be more creative. In some ways, contemporary is harder on the body than ballet; there's more floor work. I didn't know what dancing was until I came here.

What are your plans after graduation?

I am going to London on the exchange program the first semester [of my senior year]. After graduation, I am hoping to join a company that pays well and travels, and will let me be creative, allow the dancer to manipulate the choreography. Maybe Netherlands Dance Theater, Stuttgart, Hubbard Street . . .

Center Stage *profile*

Name: Jodie Gates
Job: Dancer, Joffrey Ballet Company and Pennsylvania Ballet; professor of dance, and now vice dean of Glorya Kaufman School of Dance at USC (University of Southern California)

What will you offer your students?

Ballet, jazz, and hip-hop. Ballet gives a base to work off of and a strong sense of articulation. Hip-hop is huge. There are several different ideas as to what hip-hop is [based on] your location . . . . It is highly influenced by the music of today. It is urban contemporary dance using isolation and control, and is so much a part of our culture. Hip-hop will be a part of the curriculum.

There has been a monumental shift (in attitude) among professionals and youngsters deciding to go to college. It is more acceptable in the dance world to go to college. There are professional dancers going back to school in their forties to get an MFA. What do the dance students today need to get a job in five years? Where do we want our graduates to be placed in the work force? Not just as a performer but [in] administration, choreography, or teaching. We'll be different than the others, adding to the renaissance in dance. The crossover between ballet and modern started a new type of company, different types of bodies and styles. It's an amazing mix—a new classification of dance. We will be a new footprint.

Name: Stephen Koplowitz
Job: Dean of the California Institute of the Arts (CalArts) Dance Department

What do you offer your students?

Our students get the highest quality of education. All our resources go to our students. Our student body in the dance department has between eighty-five and ninety-three students, including the MFAs [Masters of Fine Arts candidates]. The student-to-faculty ratio is high. Our students get the highest quality of instruction and personal attention.

Our students have diverse backgrounds and are of different sizes and shapes. We encourage individual creativity, but we don't shun the marketplace. CalArts sees the importance of students getting jobs. Times and economy change. Our focus is toward a career in the twenty-first century—what is happening *now*. The more [the students] know what is out there, the more they can plan a career.

We focus on preparing them with vigorous training and planned programming. We are interested in our students staying in the field longer, so we give them a full measure of experience in all aspects of the art form: lighting design, sound design, stage management, video editing. We have a strong liberal arts program, including Critical Studies; you have to be able to communicate. You will not have a career if you cannot write.

Choosing What's Right for You

There are literally *hundreds* of colleges, universities, and conservatories for you to consider along with many factors:

Do I want to stay close to home or go a substantial distance?

Do I want to be on a large campus or a small one?

What connections to the professional world are offered by the school?

What are the credentials of the faculty? Have they worked professionally in the business or spent all of their careers in academia?

What kind of facilities does the school offer?

Whichever schools you are considering, you should arrange for a campus visit before making a decision. One way to do this is through a summer intensive program, where you will remain on campus for a full week or more. This will really give you a good idea about whether or not you want to spend four years there.

All right, truth or consequences time: Will a college degree help you get a Broadway gig or get accepted into a dance company? No, not directly. As Nick Duran pointed out about the group of dancers within which he moves in LA, he is the only one with a college degree. However, there are so many life lessons that you will learn in college outside the prescribed curriculum that it will be invaluable when you go out into the world and start competing for work. After four years in college, you will be more grounded, more confident, and no, you will not be "too old."

Can you go to college after your dance career? Sure. But you might find that a more difficult road, as you will have more responsibilities weighing on you when you are older—money and family, psychological and emotional. It can be done, but it is a different game when you are over thirty than when you are eighteen. Also consider that a dancer's career lasts longer now than

READING, WRITING, AND ARITHMETIC + DANCE = THREE SCHOOL OPTIONS

It takes countless hours in the studio in front of the mirror to make the difficult look easy. How do kids do it?

Some work their dance training around their academics by attending a "regular" school and then heading to the studio immediately afterward.

Others attend performing arts schools like La Guardia High School in New York, made famous in the movie *Fame*. These professional schools balance their students' academic classes with their dance training.

Some are homeschooled, taking their academic requirements online and finding it easier to work their academics around their dance training, rather than the other way around.

Each of these approaches can and does work; it just depends on what will work best for *you*.

it did a generation ago. People in general have longer life spans, and dancers know more about their bodies and how to take care of them. A shining example is Wendy Whelan, principal dancer with NYCB. Her career with that company has spanned over twenty-seven years. You have time.

College programs also offer internships. Usually, you have to do an internship in a related field as a requirement for your degree. And internships give you the advantage of making connections. Some dance companies allow the interns to take company class. That is a terrific way to be seen and possibly considered. And don't discount the benefit of rubbing elbows with staff. This kind of exposure to the different areas of company life will broaden your horizons and should get you thinking about what else you might be interested in doing down the road.

No matter what career path you chose in life, you should always have a "plan B." If you want to be a dancer, your plan B is not a "cheat," it is a necessity. The answer to the college question is as individual as you are. Look at all your options and weigh your alternatives.

How to Convince Your Parents That a Performing Career is Right for You[3]

Catie Kovelman is sixteen, takes AP classes in high school, wants a career in Broadway musicals, and is looking at colleges offering a Musical Theater program. "Every college I look at, I look at their arts programs," said Catie. "I like all parts of the industry."

Her father wants her to go to medical school. "I've been singing and doing musicals since I was six. My parents thought it was a phase, so they let me do it—for now."

Catie applied to Brown University's musical-theater summer intensive program. She auditioned on video, singing "On My Own" from *Les Miserables* and performing a dramatic monologue. She was accepted and given a scholarship to attend the six-week program. Instead, her father insisted she go to Washington, DC, to participate in a medical program for high school students thinking about a career in medicine. "I think it was his last-ditch attempt

to get me to go to medical school," she said. So rather than pursue something relating to her dream career, Catie found herself in the nation's capitol, observing a surgical procedure on a knee. She fainted. With orthopedic surgeon off the list of possible career choices, what was her next step? Catie has made her decision. But her parents . . .

"It's a constant question. 'Are you sure? Are you really sure?'" Catie said of her parents' worry. "They bring up everything that can go wrong— anything you do has an upside and a downside.

[Dance] makes me happy. I like the craft; I'm not in it for the fame or fortune. My dad wants to be sure I can support myself. I'll find ways. I'll make it work. I'll figure it out. If you want something badly enough, you will find a way."

Catie is already finding her way by networking and making connections to people in the industry. "You just don't know where anyone will be in five years," she observes. Her high school music teacher has counseled her in the "go big or go home" philosophy.

Caties's determination has paid off. Brown has already accepted her into their summer program for next year. How do her parents feel about it this time? "The more I do it, the more I wear them down," Catie says, "Just like they used to wear me down. It's been a battle; we had some shout-outs in the past."

But Caties's dad is singing a different tune these days. "Keep your options open to do what you want to do," has become his motto. "I can think for myself," Catie said. "It's my decision as to what I do."

ACTIVITY
College Resources: Divide and Conquer

The first decision is whether or not you want to apply to a college or try to get in to a company after graduating from high school. To help you answer that question, do the following:

1. Get a standard piece of paper.

2. Fold it in half lengthwise.

3. List the advantages of going to college on one side.

4. List the disadvantages, as you see them, on the other side.

5. Get another piece of paper and make the same two lists for joining a company / launching a dance career.

6. Study both, side by side.

There are college reference guides in the resources chapter. If you are really on the fence, examine the programs listed in those guides and see if any of them might provide you with additional training that would benefit you; or if any offer connections to the industry that you would not receive otherwise. It is possible to go to college *and* launch your career at the same time.

If you have made the decision to go to college, then you will certainly want to study the reference guides to explore what is available at each school and to help you narrow the field. Examine requirements carefully, as the requisites for each school will vary. Some will want you to have taken more math classes in high school than others; some will require you have taken a number of years of foreign language before applying. If you intend to go to a college or university directly from high school, there will be one set of requirements. If you attend a junior college first and then want to transfer, you will need to have accumulated a certain amount of credits, and the class requirements will be different.

1. Get another piece of paper.

2. Fold it in half.

3. List college names on the left side.

4. List requirements on the right.

5. Study the information.

6. Make an appointment with your school counselor. Your piece of paper may appear neat, but the content is complicated. Your counselor will be able to help you through the maze.

SPOTLIGHT

Susan Jaffee: From Center Stage to Corner Office

Susan Jaffee joined American Ballet Theatre in 1980. As a principal ballerina, she danced with the company for twenty years, working with such choreographers as George Balanchine, Twyla Tharp, Jerome Robbins, and Antony Tudor. She also performed with Britain's Royal Ballet, the Kirov Ballet in Russia, and La Scala Theatre Ballet in Italy. She became ballet mistress of ABT in October of 2010; she also lent her talents to the Youth America Grand Prix as artistic coordinator.

In August of 2012, she took the reins as dean of the University of North Carolina School of the Arts dance program, following in the footsteps of another ABT alum, Ethan Stiefel. Assistant Dean Brenda Daniels stated that Jaffee "really wants to focus on a more classic base of training that will allow students to take on another style."[4]

10

Looking Past the Stage Lights

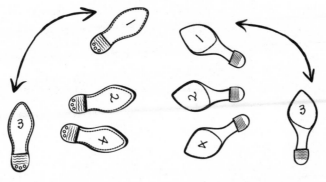

It is the question that lurks in the corners of your mind:

What will you do when you can't dance any longer?

You shove it further back every time it seeps forward into your conscious thoughts. You don't want to think about it now; your entire life has been focused on having a professional career as a dancer. You've worked hard to get here, and now that you are a professional dancer, the last thing you want to think about is the end of a career that has just begun. You continue to take class every day, plus have rehearsals in the afternoon and performances at night; you'll think about it later. As ballet major Alexis Johnson put it, "The [idea] of not doing this every day is frightening."[1] Yes it is. And for that reason you do need to think about it—now.

Name: Michelle Burch
Job: Performance teams manager for the Portland Trail Blazers

Why did you become this?

I pursued this opportunity with the Trail Blazers because it blends two things I love: Trail Blazer Basketball and *dance*! I cannot see my life without dance as part of it, whether I'm performing, teaching, choreographing, witnessing performances. Can't imagine a day without dance.

What type of education did you pursue to enter this career?

My dance training is diverse. I trained in jazz, ballet, tap, modern, hip-hop, and African disciplines. I started dancing at Broadwell's Dance Studio when I was six years old and never stopped, continuing on to programs like the dance magnet at Harriet Tubman Middle School and then Jefferson High School and the Jefferson Dancers. I also danced in college. Probably most significantly, I was also a BlazerDancer for six seasons. My professional experience comes from my bachelor of science in communications.

Who helped you further your career in this field?

I think all of my dance training helped prepare me for [my] career because it gave me such a broad and solid foundation in the arts. My parents have been incredibly encouraging and supportive of [my] finding a way to pursue a career that includes my love of dance and the arts. I've also had encouragement from Dee Dee Anderson who was my coach as a BlazerDancer, and she continues to be a great resource to me.

What type of work or volunteer experiences helped you gain the contacts you need to achieve your career goals?
I believe that I built a solid reputation for myself as a hard worker beyond my talent as a dancer. I am professional at all times and in all situations. I think having a good reputation speaks volumes about a person. I certainly think it helped me enter a highly competitive industry. Willingness to learn was also important for me. Most of my professional experience is in the nonprofit world. I had many opportunities to volunteer with my students all over the city of Portland, and [am] grateful and humbled by the various experiences.

What is the most difficult part of your job?
Auditions are the most difficult part of my job. We host them each year and everyone has to audition, even if they have already been on the team. Emotions run high for everyone through the process, and that includes me. We make every effort to select the best ambassadors for the Trail Blazers, but in that process, I know people are disappointed . . . That is a harsh reality. Tough decisions.

What is the most rewarding part of your job?
So many things are rewarding about the job. While auditions are tough, they are also exhilarating when I have an opportunity to greet my new team for the first time in person. The crazy excitement in the room is matched by no other experience all year. Watching them perform together on opening night in the Moda Center is another highlight. We rarely have everyone working a game, so having all sixteen dancers out there with the excitement of the fans is pretty amazing.

What advice would you give to kids interested in this work?
Dance as much as you can. Study multiple styles to become a well-rounded artist. Be dedicated to your craft and your goals. It is competitive, but it is attainable. Put yourself in a position

to be successful—attend clinics and junior camps put on by pro and semipro teams. Ask for feedback and internalize the constructive criticisms. People can't deny improvement, and that speaks to your dedication and work ethic.

When you were a kid, did you think you would enter this profession?
When I was young, I just knew that I would always dance. That was all I knew. I never imagined I would have an opportunity to have dance be the focal point of my professional career. I'm beyond thankful for this opportunity.

A CHORUS LINE BIG ANNIVERSARY

On the evening of September 23, 1983, *A Chorus Line* celebrated a very special milestone: the show was to play its 3,389th performance, making it the longest-running Broadway show of all time to that date. For this landmark performance, 250 dancers who had done the show were flown in to New York to work with creator Michael Bennett. For the next week, Bennett happily went to work restaging the show to accommodate the original cast times ten in preparation for the historic performance.

The air was electric that autumn night. The names of every cast member who had danced in *A Chorus Line* scrolled across the famous ticker tape in Times Square.[2] Celebrities and press crowded into Shubert Alley. Never before had there been such excitement and anticipation before a performance of a Broadway musical; all of Broadway had come to celebrate the event. They weren't disappointed. Bennett's restaging was so cleverly done that it was difficult to imagine the show *not* being done with 250 people. The finale was explosive, with dancers spotlighted throughout the theater as well as onstage, high-kicking and singing their way through the "One" sequence, then swarming the stage with the energy of a tsunami tidal wave. It was at once exhilarating, nostalgic, and bittersweet, as everyone knew this moment would never come again.

More Than You Imagined

Alex Castillo, soloist with Los Angeles Ballet, has his eye on teaching when he decides to back gracefully offstage. "With my career, I just want to take it day by day," he said. "I was just promoted to soloist. I feel like I have a path and what will happen will happen. I would love to dance in Europe at the end of my career. I would really love to teach at Ballet Academy East [in New York] and give back. I owe them everything, and I won't be complete until I have given back."[3]

Then there are those who are still performing but have actively begun the process of transitioning to the second career. Allynne Noelle, principal ballerina with Los Angeles Ballet, was blindsided by a foot injury. She suffered an identity crisis when she realized that there was a chance she might not be able to dance again, and she began to think about the next step.

"I tried to cut out ballet after the injury," she said. "What do I want to do now? It was hard to conceptualize. I have maybe two to five years left. I would still like the opportunity of dancing in Europe—The Royal Ballet, Béjart Ballet Lausanne, Stuttgart. I am in college part-time now through a program offered by St. Mary's College designed to assist professional performing artists in getting their degree. But 'ballerina' will always be a part of my life."[4] She is now thinking about a career in medicine.

HOW TO BECOME LUVABULL

Here's the schedule for a recent audition for the Luvabulls, the Chicago Bulls basketball team dance squad:

SATURDAY
8:00 AM: Doors open
8:45 AM: Doors close

Round 1

★ Candidates freestyle dance to music that the judges provide. Dance ability is number one on the list of requirements to be a Luvabull.

★ Judges make cuts.

★ Judges interview candidates in groups of twenty. Energy, enthusiasm, and poise are also on the list of attributes a sports-team dancer must have.

★ Judges make cuts.

Lunch: Thirty minutes, and you must bring all your own food and drinks.

Round 2

★ Candidates are taught a routine and then perform it.

★ Judges make the final selection of thirty to forty dancers who will move forward to training camp

MONDAY–WEDNESDAY

Just two days after the first day of auditions, the small group of remaining hopefuls must continue to prove themselves in three days of training. Not all of them will make the final cut. And remember, they're dancing after a long day at work, and each training day lasts from 6:30–10:00 PM.

Gwen Verdon:
A Star from Age Six

Gwen Verdon started her dance training early, thanks to her mother, who was a Denishawn dancer. By the time Verdon was six years old, she was already working in variety shows. When the choreographer Jack Cole came to MGM, he chose her to be his assistant.

A talented dancer, she could certainly sing and act as well, winning four Tony Awards and six nominations. Her first major success was in the original Broadway production of *Can Can*, where, even in a supporting role, she stole the show. Leading roles followed after that, the most notable being Lola in *Damn Yankees* (both on Broadway and in film), Charity in *Sweet Charity* on Broadway, and that merry murderess Roxie Hart in *Chicago* on Broadway, all choreographed by Bob Fosse.

Having met while working on *Damn Yankees*, Gwen Verdon and Bob Fosse married and continued to work together. Even after they separated twenty-seven years later, Verdon assisted Fosse in casting and advising him on his shows.

Verdon's last appearance was in the movie *Cocoon*, directed by Ron Howard.

Dancers can be very inventive when it comes to developing their second careers. Certain experiences and frustrations they have had while performing open up entirely new avenues. Here are some examples:

Marisa Cerveris, dancewear designer, was a former dancer with New York City Ballet who became frustrated by how her leotards fit—or didn't. At her costume fittings, she paid close attention to the conversations between NYCB artistic director Peter Martins and costume builder Barbara Matera. She started forming her own ideas as to how a dancer's wardrobe should fit. "My approach to designing dancewear is the same as my approach to being a dancer—line is most important. I am basically trying to paint the body with fabric,"[5] she said in an interview with *Dance Teacher* magazine. Her ByMarisa dancewear line has led her to designing for the Robert Altman' film *Company* (based on the Joffrey) as well as TV's *Dancing with the Stars*.

Phil La Duca, footwear designer, danced in the National Company of *A Chorus Line*, among many other Broadway shows, and saw the need to keep a dancer's feet happy. He developed his own line of flexible footwear, La Duca Shoes, based in New York. Now known as the "wizard of showbiz footwear,"[6] his shoes have been worn by such celebrities as Katy Perry, Kristen Chenowith, Brooke Shields, Catherine Zeta-Jones, and Meryl Streep. His footwear is in high demand on both the Broadway stage and the Hollywood film studio.

Jennifer Paulson Lee, cosmetics entrepreneur, could not get her mascara to cooperate as she tried to apply it before a performance of *Wonderful Town* in New York. "I couldn't get the look I wanted for the time period of the production."[7] So Lee developed her own mascara and patented delivery system. LashControl is available in spas, boutiques, and online. "As a dancer, you often feel if you do something other than dance, you are abandoning yourself and your art. But I've learned [that] it's essential to allow yourself to be many different things."[8] she told *Dance Teacher* magazine.

Robert Small, landscape designer, "had never really focused on the future," he said in an interview with *Dance Teacher* magazine. "I was still so happy being a dancer. I loved everything about it."[9] So when a friend asked him what he was going to do after his dancing career, he had no answer. That same friend gave him a brochure for landscape design, and nine years later, Small enrolled in a landscape design course. He then became an apprentice to a professional designer and worked with him for five years before striking out on his own. Small found his dance career provided the skills necessary for his new career to thrive. "All those years of meeting new people and thinking on your feet. For the first time, I feel that I'm fully in charge of my own life."[10]

Kelly Bishop danced in many Broadway musicals and won a Tony Award for her performance as Sheila in the original cast of *A Chorus Line*. She is probably best known now for her role as dance teacher Fanny Flowers in ABC Family's *Bunheads*. Schooled by her mother, Bishop started her ballet training at age six in Denver, Colorado. She then transferred to a satellite school of American Ballet Theatre. When she turned eighteen, she moved to New York, expecting to be accepted into ABT. But that didn't happen. In need of a job, Bishop became a member of the Radio City Music Hall corps de ballet, dancing four shows a day. Later, she was able to find steady work as a Broadway dancer, which eventually led to the featured role in *A Chorus Line*. Bishop transitioned into an acting career in Los Angeles and is usually cast in the "domineering mother" roles, which she played successfully in TV shows like *Gilmore Girls*.

Charlton Boyd, massage therapist, danced with the Mark Morris Dance Group for fourteen years. After a knee injury and three surgical procedures, he took a leave of absence from the rigors of daily life in a dance company to figure out his next move. "As anyone in concert dance knows, company life . . . can be all consuming. It's a vicious cycle of constant wear on the body and psyche,"[11] he said in an interview with *Dance Teacher* magazine. His dance training having given him a thorough understanding of anatomy, body mechanics, and energy flow, Boyd decided to become a massage therapist. He completed a program at the Swedish Institute (in New York), became licensed, and then worked at a private spa before going into private practice.

DANCER BRAVES CANNIBALS IN AMAZON JUNGLE

Jack Cole first studied with Ruth St. Denis at Denishawn. There, he learned St. Denis's brand of East Indian dancing, but Cole wanted authenticity—not only dance steps but cultures. He explored Native American, African American, and Caribbean cultures, studying what they wore, how they lived. So intense was his drive for authenticity, he ventured into the Amazon jungle, enduring intense heat, huge insects, and cannibalistic tribes in an effort to study the dances of the local people. That trip proved less than successful in his mind. As he described it: "What did the natives wear? Dirty G-strings! How did they dance? A rotten shuffle! Oog-oog-unka to the right. Oog-oog-unka to the left. And for this I risked my neck?"[12] Back on safer ground, Cole was hired by Columbia Pictures in 1944 to create the first permanent dance company for a film studio. He started with twelve dancers, working them a grueling six hours a day, training them to be prepared for anything and everything that could be asked of them on a set. They became the most skilled dance troupe in film at that time. Each dancer was well paid, and at least one third of them became stars—Gwen Verdon being one. Cole's choreographic style can be seen in the works of Gower Champion and Bob Fosse.

In the Wings *profile*

Name: Paige Hart
Age: 16
Job (when not studying!): Ballet student
Dream job: Undecided

When did you start dancing and why?
I was four years old. My mother took me to see *The Nutcracker* that my current studio is producing. I was completely mesmerized and had to start right away. My mom said that after the show, all I wanted to do was talk to and see the ballerinas.

Why did you decide to audition for the School of American Ballet Summer Intensive?
It makes me work harder. I danced Odette's variation from the second act of *Swan Lake*. Having to work on one variation and perfect it is a great experience.

How do you feel about being required to take a class in the contemporary style of dance as part of your ballet training?
It's a looser version of ballet. We also do Broadway stuff. It's a lot of fun.

How do you fit school into all of this?
Ballet class helps a lot—working out before homework. I have more brain power.

What will you do after high school?
I haven't decided if I'm going to pursue dance or not. I know what I want to do, I just don't know how. I don't know where it's going to take me. You have to fly by the seat of your pants, and that's scary. I'll probably take the educational route in psychology or sociology. I'm thinking about NYU.

What about your social life? What do your friends think about your dancing?
I think my friends at school have given up. My friends are here at the studio.

Tina Landon:
Pop Girl with Depth

Tina Landon began her career as a Laker Girl. She then toured as a dancer with Janet Jackson in the Rhythm Nation 1814 Tour and began her career as a choreographer staging both the Janet World Tour and The Velvet Rope Tour, for which she received an Emmy nomination for Outstanding Achievement in Choreography. In 2000, Jennifer Lopez, one of Landon's former dancers, presented the Mexican-American choreographer with the American Latino Media Arts (ALMA) Award for Achievement in Choreography. Landon has choreographed for Rhianna, and teaches master classes at the Millennium Dance Complex in Los Angeles and the Triple Threat Dance Convention in Canada.

Looking Down the Road

Of course, right now, all you want to do is dance, and that is as it should be. But it is a good idea to think down the road about what your next move will be. Having some options on the back burner will make matters easier. When the time comes to exit the stage, you may want to contact Career Transitions for Dancers. With offices in New York, Los Angeles, and Chicago, CTD stands ready to assist you, with individual counseling, guidance, and funding for dancers who have decided it's time to change directions and go down a different road. Every fall, Career Transitions for Dancers holds a gala in New York to raise the funds necessary for the organization to provide its many services, which include online assistance, grants, and scholarships. Founded in 1985, the organization has helped some five thousand dancers take the last bow of their dance careers and make a graceful entrance into another equally rewarding career.

Dancers are a breed apart. Dancers do not approach or go through the world in the same manner as other performing artists—or anyone else, for that matter. Dancers are exceptionally disciplined, determined, and tenacious, always striving for perfection and willing to do whatever it takes to get the job done. As retiring musical theater dancer John Williford put it, "Dancers are different. There is a certain 'wonderlust' in us you never lose. You breathe dance. Look to the excitement of tomorrow and not the loss of yesterday. You will always be a dancer."[13]

11

Resources

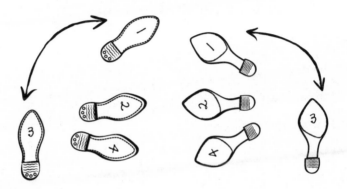

Books and Magazines

Basic Principles of Classical Ballet by Aggrippina Vaganova (Dover Publications, 2012)

Dance Anatomy by Jacque Greene Haas (Human Kinetics, 2010)

Dance Magazine, dancemagazine.com

Dance Spirit, dancespirit.com

Dance Teacher, dance-teacher.com

The Healthy Dancer: ABT Guidelines for Dancer Health by the ABT Medical Advisory Board (McFadden Performing Arts Media, 2008)

How Does the Show Go On by Thomas Schumacker and Jeff Kurtti (Disney Editions, 2007)

Pointe, pointemagazine.com

The Pointe Book: Shoes, Training, Technique by Janice Barringer and Sarah Schlesinger (Princeton Book Company, 2012)

To a Young Dancer by Agnes De Mille (Little Brown & Company, 1962)

Dance Companies with Youth and Community Programs

Alvin Ailey American Dance Theater, alvinailey.org

American Ballet Theatre, abt.org

Ballet Hispanico, ballethispanico.org

Body Traffic, bodytraffic.com

Boston Ballet, bostonballet.org

Central Pennsylvania Youth Ballet, cpyb.org

Dance Theatre of Harlem, dancetheatreofharlem.org

Houston Ballet, houstonballet.org

Hubbard Street Dance Chicago, hubbardstreetdance.com

Joffrey Ballet, joffrey.com

José Limón Dance Company, limon.org

Martha Graham Center of Contemporary Dance, marthagraham.org

New York City Ballet, nycballet.com

Paul Taylor Dance Company, ptdc.org

Documentaries

Ballets Russes. Daniel Geller and Dayna Goldfine, directors. 2005.

Broadway or Bust. PBS. 2012.

Broadway: The American Musical. PBS. 2004.

Every Little Step. Adam Del Deo and James D. Stern, directors. 2008.

First Position. Bess Kargman, director. 2011.

Dancemaker. Matthew Diamond, director. 1998.

"Jerome Robbins: Something to Dance About." Judy Kinberg, director. *American Masters*, PBS. 2009.

Joffrey: Mavericks of American Dance. Bob Hercules, director. 2012.

That's Entertainment! Jack Haley, Jr., director. 1974.

That's Entertainment, Part II. Gene Kelly, director. 1976.

That's Entertainment! III. Bud Friedgen and Michael J. Sheridan, directors. 1994.

Education and Job Resources

Backstage, backstage.com (career advice and casting info)

Broadway Dance Center, broadwaydancecenter.com

Dance Magazine College Guide, http://www.dancemagazine.com/thecollegeguide/

Dance Magazine Scholarship Guide 2013, http://www.dancemagazine.com/images/DMscholarshipguide_0813.pdf

Dance Teacher Magazine Higher-Ed Guide, dance-teacher.com (released in every September issue)

Dance Theatre of Harlem School, http://www.dancetheatreofharlem.org/school/index.html

Dance U 101, www.danceu101.com

Hubbard Street Dance Chicago, http://www.hubbardstreetdance.com /index.php?option=com_content&view=article&id=92&Itemid=48

Summer Programs and Camps

Dance Teacher Magazine Summer Study Guide, dance-teacher.com (released in every January issue)

Disney Youth Performing Arts Programs, http://www.disney youth.com/our-programs/performing-arts/

US Performing Arts Camps, usperformingarts.com

Also check out your local community centers, high schools, and colleges for summer dance programs.

12

glossary

act. The dramatic action is divided into sections called acts.

AEA. Actors' Equity Association—the union governing actors and dancers who work in professional (live) theater productions.

AGMA. Amercian Guild of Musical Artists—the union governing musicians and dancers appearing in concert or ballet productions.

ballad. A slow song or slow part of a musical piece.

balletti. The original Italian word for *ballet*.

bar. A small section of music, also known as a measure.

barre. The railing a dancer hangs on to when they begin a dance class.

battement. A small or large kick.

book. The script of a Broadway musical.

bus and truck. A rigorous touring schedule where the company travels in a bus and the sets are moved in a truck.

call the time. Time at which a dancer is scheduled to be at a rehearsal or performance.

cattle call. An audition which is attended by a large number of people, usually hundreds, being herded through the audition process like cattle.

center. A dancer's center of gravity by which he or she balances.

center work. Dancing in the middle of the studio floor, away from the barre.

choreographer. A person who creates dances.

corps de ballet. The chorus in a ballet company.

crossover. A number or scene which takes place in front of a curtain or scrim while the set is being changed behind it.

danseur. A male dancer.

danseuse. A female dancer.

downbeat. The gesture the conductor of an orchestra makes to signal the musicians to start playing.

en pointe. Dancing in pointe shoes.

from the top. The command given by a director, choreographer, or conductor to start a number again from the beginning.

gel. A colored film placed over a lighting instrument to create different colors onstage according to the lighting designer's design.

gig. A job.

grand pirouette. A turn on one foot with the opposite leg extended to the side at a right angle to the hip (second position). Most often done by men in their variations.

gypsy. A Broadway chorus dancer.

house. The place in the theater where the audience sits.

IATSE. International Association of Theatrical and Stage Employees—the union for stagehands working in professional theater, television, and film.

line. The pictures a dancer paints with his or her body.

line. The words an actor speaks in a musical (or straight play).

minstrel show. A variety show performed with an African American chorus of adults and children.

national company. A touring company of a Broadway show, playing only major cities.

parody. A song that uses different words than the original lyrics but the same music.

pas de deux. Literally translated as "dance of two," or partner work in ballet.

pick-up band or dancers. Local musicians or dancers employed to work in a show for the duration of a limited run in that city.

pit. The recessed area in front of the stage where the orchestra sits.

plié. A small or deep bending of the knees.

pointe shoes. Shoes used in ballet by the ballerina that are constructed to enable her to dance on her toes.

protégé. A young person with talent being mentored by an established artist.

SAG/AFTRA. Screen Actors' Guild / Amercian Federation of Television and Radio Artists—the union (formerly two) which governs actors in these mediums.

scale. The minimum salary for a dancer performing in a ballet, dance concert, or Broadway show.

score. The music of a ballet, concert dance, or Broadway show.

show bible. The stage manger's notebook, which contains the cues needed to run the show as well as some notes.

SSDC. Society of Stage Directors and Choreographers—the union governing these postions.

technique. The way a dancer performs steps.

tempo. How fast or slow the music is played.

Tony Award. Named for Antoinette Perry (actress, director, producer, and American Theatre Wing cofounder), the Tony Awards are held every June to honor the best performances on Broadway for a specific season. The stage equivalent of the Academy Awards (the Oscars) for film or the Emmy Awards for television.

tour. Traveling from one city to the next for performances.

tour en l'air. A vertical jump where the dancer goes straight up and turns once or twice in the air before landing.

understudy. A person, usually in the chorus, who learns a lead role and is ready to perform it should the lead be ill, injured, or on vacation.

virtuoso. An extraordinarily gifted and talented artist.

NOTES

Chapter 1

1. Jennifer Homans, *Apollo's Angels* (New York: Random House, 2010), 61.
2. Jocelyn Noveck, "David Hallberg: How He Went from South Dakota to the Bolshoi," *The Huffington Post*, November 3, 2011, http://www.huffingtonpost.com /2011/11/03/david-hallberg-bolshoi_n_1073380.html.
3. Ibid.
4. Arlene Croce, "Balanchine Said," *The New Yorker*, January 26, 2009, http://www.newyorker.com /reporting/2009/01/26/090126fa_fact_croce.
5. Robert Joffrey, interviewed by April Daly, *Joffrey: Mavericks of American Dance*, directed by Bob Hercules, aired December 28, 2012 (Chicago: Lakeview Films, 2012), DVD.
6. Linda Hamilton, "Advice for Dancers: Stop Panicking Every Meal," *Dance Magazine*, June 2013, http:// www.dancemagazine.com/issues/June-2013/ Advice-for-Dancers-Stop-Panicking-Every-Meal.

Chapter 2

1. Robert Joffrey, interviewed by April Daly, *Joffrey: Mavericks of American Dance*, directed by Bob Hercules, aired December 28, 2012 (Chicago: Lakeview Films, 2012), DVD.

2. "Dance in America: Dance Theatre of Harlem," *Great Performances*, PBS, aired 1977.

3. Maureen Callahan, "Dancer Misty Copeland Has Broken Barriers to Bring Ballet Center Stage," *New York Post*, June 2, 2013, http://nypost.com/2013/06/02 /dancer-misty-copeland-has-broken-barriers-to-bring -ballet-center-stage/.

4. "Dance in America."

5. Debra Levine, "Talking with Dance Theatre of Harlem's Co-founder Arthur Mitchell," *Los Angeles Times,* July 6, 2010, http://latimesblogs.latimes.com /culturemonster /2010/07/talking-with-dance-theatre-of -harlems-legendary-dancer-arthur-mitchell.html.

6. Ibid.

7. Mike Fritz and Tom Legro, "Amid Turmoil, American 'Prince' David Hallberg Returns to Russia," PBS NewsHour, July 1, 2013, http://www.pbs.org/newshour /art/dancer-david-hallberg/.

Chapter 3

1. Gerald Bordman, *American Musical Theatre: A Chronicle* (New York: Oxford University Press, 1978), 18–20.

2. Ibid.

3. Jocelyn Noveck, "David Hallberg: How He Went from South Dakota to the Bolshoi," *The Huffington Post*, November 3, 2011, http://www.huffingtonpost.com /2011/11/03/david-hallberg-bolshoi_n_1073380.html.

4. Richard Kislan, *Hoofing It on Broadway* (New York: Prentiss Hall, 1987), 111.

5. Gower Champion, interviewed by Tom Dixon, *Luncheon at the Music Center*, KFAC Los Angeles, 1977.

6. Sam Wasserson, *Fosse* (Boston: Houghton, Mifflin, Harcourt, 2013), 53.

7. Kislan, *Hoofing It*, 117.

8. Kristin Schwab, "Technique: TaraMarie Perri," *Dance*

Teacher, August 1, 2013, http://www.dance-teacher
.com/2013/08/technique-taramarie-perri/.

Chapter 4

1. Ann Daly, *Done into Dance: Isadora Duncan in America* (Middletown, CT: Wesleyan University Press, 2010), 30.
2. Walter Terry, *Miss Ruth: The "More Living Life" of Ruth St. Denis* (New York: Dodd, Mead, and Company, 1969), 6.
3. Ibid., 21.
4. Ibid., 48.
5. Ibid., 77.
6. Martha Graham, *Blood Memory: An Autobiography* (New York: Doubleday, 1991), 67.
7. "Chronology of José Limón and the José Limón Dance Foundation," José Limón Dance Foundation, accessed April 1, 2014, http://limon.org/about-us/founders /chronology/.
8. "About Alvin Ailey American Dance Theater," Alvin Ailey American Dance Theater, accessed April 1, 2014, http://www.alvinailey.org/about?gclid=CMfO_baBobk CFUXhQgodDkkA3Q.
9. "Paul Taylor," *American Masters*, PBS, aired October 8, 2001.
10. Jen Jones Donatelli, "Lyrical Out Loud," *Dance Teacher*, December 1, 2012, http://www.dance-teacher.com /2012/12/lyrical-out-loud/.
11. Kristin Schwab, "Face to Face: From the Heartland to the Orient," *Dance Teacher*, December 23, 2011, http://www .dance-teacher.com/2010/06/technique-marty-kudelka/.
12. Kenya Clay, as observed by author during a class at the Millennium Dance Complex (Los Angeles), July 13, 2013.
13. Alison Feller, "High Five with Cris Judd," *Dance Teacher*, November 30, 2011, http://www.dance-teacher.com /2011/11/high-five-with-cris-judd/.
14. Nick Duran, commercial dancer, interview with author, April 2013.

Chapter 5

1. Jenny Dalzell, "Technique: Marty Kudelka," *Dance Teacher*, June 1, 2010, http://www.dance-teacher.com /2010/06/technique-marty-kudelka/.
2. Author's experience as an agent; Jen Jones Donatelli, "Getting an Agent," *Dance Spirit*, December 6, 2012, http://www.dancespirit.com/2012/12/getting-an-agent/.
3. Lauren Kay, "Nathanial Hathaway: Broadway Wig Supervisor," *Beyond Performance*, November 30, 2012, 18.
4. Ibid.

Chapter 6

1. Allynne Noelle, interview with author, April 2013.
2. Lauren Kay, "Technique My Way: Ray Mercer," *Dance Magazine*, August 2013, http://www.dancemagazine.com /issues/August-2013/Technique-My-Way-Ray-Mercer.
3. Ibid.
4. Kathleen McGuire, "The Good, the Bad, and the Ugly," *Dance Teacher*, September 30, 2011, http://www.dance -teacher.com/2011/09/the-good-the-bad-and-the-ugly/.
5. Elena Hecht, "Technique My Way: Julia Burrer," *Dance Magazine*, May 2013, http://www.dancemagazine.com /issues/May-2013/Technique-My-Way-Julia-Burrer.
6. Sheryl Baxter, interview with author, May 2013.
7. Corrinne Glover, interview with author, April 2013.
8. Erica Sobol, interview with author, May 2013.

Chapter 7

1. Leslie Holleran, "Angela Sterling: Ballet Photographer," *Beyond Performance*, November 30, 2012, 4.
2. *Entertainment Weekly*, review of *Apollo's Angels*, quoted in Jennifer Homans, *Apollo's Angels: A History of Ballet* (New York: Random House, 2011), iii.

3. "The 2010 Pulitzer Prize Winners: Criticism," The Pulitzer Prizes, accessed September 29, 2013, http://www.pulitzer .org/citation/2010-Criticism.

4. Sarah Kaufman, "2010 Pulitzer Prize: Sarah Kaufman on Winning Criticism, Role of Arts Coverage," *The Washington Post*, April 14, 2010, http://www.washingtonpost.com/wp-dyn/content /discussion/2010/04/13/DI2010041303523.html.

5. Alastair Macaulay, "Timeless Alchemy, Even When No One Is Dancing," *New York Times*, November 28, 2010, http://www.nytimes.com/2010/11/29/arts/dance /29nutcracker.html.

6. "Confessions of a Dance Critic," *Pointe*, December 2011/ January 2012, http://www.pointemagazine.com/issues /december-2011january-2012/confessions-dance-critic.

7. Gelsey Kirkland and Greg Lawrence, *Dancing on My Grave* (New York: Doubleday & Company, 1986), 205.

Chapter 8

1. Astrida Woods, "A Flairr for the Dramatic," *Dance Magazine*, July 2013, http://www.dancemagazine.com /issues/June-2013/A-flair-for-the-dramatic.

2. Ibid.

Chapter 9

1. Brenda Daniels, interview with author, June 2013.

2. Ibid.

3. Catie Kovelman, interview with author, July 2013.

4. Brenda Daniels, interview with author, June 2013.

Chapter 10

1. Alexis Johnson, interview with author, July 2013.

2. As experienced by the author, who danced in this performance and whose name was among those that scrolled across the ticker tape.

3. Alex Castillo, interview with author, April 2013.

4. Allynne Noel, interview with author, April 2013.

5. Steve Sucato, "Marisa Cerveris: Dancewear Designer," *Beyond Performance*, September 2010, 18.

6. Phil La Duca, interview with author, August 2013.

7. Lauren Kay, "Jennifer Paulson Lee: Entrepreneur," *Beyond Performance*, September 2012, 10.

8. Ibid.

9. Linda Tarnay, "Robert Small: Landscape Designer," *Beyond Performance*, September 2011, 20.

10. Ibid.

11. Rachel Berman, "Charlton Boyd: Massage Therapist," *Beyond Performance*, September 2010, http://www .danceu101.com/articles/2010-09-01/beyond -performance-charlton-boyd-massage-therapist.

12. Richard Kislan, *Hoofing It on Broadway* (New York: Prentiss Hall, 1987), 87.

13. John Williford, interview with author, July 2013.

BIBLIOGRAPHY

Articles and Blogs

"The 2010 Pulitzer Prize Winners: Criticism." Accessed September 29, 2013. www.pulitzer.org/citation/2010-Criticism.

"2013–14 Hawks Cheerleaders Go to China." NBA.com. Accessed January 16, 2014. www.nba.com/hawks/gallery /2013-14-hawks-cheerleaders-go-china.

"About Luna Negra Dance Theater." Luna Negra Dance Theater. Accessed August 7, 2013. lunanegra.org/about/index.html.

"Alvin Ailey." Biography.com. Accessed August 28, 2013. www.biography.com/people/alvin-ailey-9177959#awesm =~oB377LoYYEJkQs.

Berman, Rachel. "Charlton Boye: Massage Therapist." *Beyond Performance*, September 2010. www.danceu101.com/articles/2010 -09-01/beyond-performance-charlton-boyd-massage-therapist.

"Black Swan: The 5 Most Influential Black Ballerinas." RollingOut.com, April 24, 2012. rollingout.com/culture /black-swan-the-5-most-influential-black-ballerinas/.

Brandt, Amy. "Pointe Shoe Primer for the 21st Century." *Dance Teacher*, August 2013, 76.

Burke, Siobhan. "Dance in the Ivy League." *Dance Magazine*, August 2013, 33–35.

"Confessions of a Dance Critic." *Pointe*, December 2011/ January 2012. www.pointemagazine.com/issues/december -2011january-2012/confessions-dance-critic.

Conner, Lynner and Susan Gillis-Kruman. "Ruth St. Denis (1879– 1968)." The Early Moderns web tutorial. University of Pittsburgh. Accessed July 27, 2013. www.pitt.edu/_gillis/dance/ruth.html.

"Contemporary Dance." *Wikipedia*. Accessed July 11, 2013. en.wikipedia.org/wiki/Contemporary_dance.

"Contemporary Dance History." Contemporary Dance History website. Accessed July 21, 2013. www.contemporary-dance .org/contemporary-dance-history.html.

Crompton, Sarah. "The Mighty Pina Bausch." *The Telegraph*. June 11, 2012. www.telegraph.co.uk/culture/theatre /dance/9272080/The-mighty-Pina-Bausch.html.

Crompton, Sarah. "William Forsythe Interview: *Artifact* is an Ode to Ballet." *The Telegraph Media*, April 18, 2012. www .telegraph.co.uk/culture/theatre/dance/9211413/William -Forsythe-interview-Artifact-is-an-ode-to-ballet.html.

Dalzell, Jenny. "Damian Woetzel, Raising the Bar for Arts Education." *Dance Teacher*, August 2010, 46.

Dalzell, Jenny. "Technique: Susan Jaffe." *Dance Teacher*, August 2010, 61.

Dawson, Lois. "The SM Prompt Book: Show Bible Pt. 1," *Lois Backstage* (blog). July 26, 2010. www.loisbackstage.com/?p=733.

Dawson, Lois. "'You've Got Everything in There!': The SM Kit," *Lois Backstage* (blog). October 5, 2009. www.loisbackstage.com/?p=323.

DeFrantz, Thomas F. "Alvin Ailey." Great Performances: Free to Dance. Accessed August 28, 2013. www.pbs.org/wnet /freetodance/biographies/ailey.html.

Fritz, Mike and Tom Legro. "American Prince David Hallberg Returns to Russia." *PBS Newshour*, July 1, 2013. www.pbs .org/newshour/art/blog/2013/07/dancer-david-hallberg.html.

Fuhrer, Margaret. "Show and Tell: Inside Ashley Murphy's Dance Bag." *Pointe*, August/September 2013. www.pointemagazine .com/issues/augustseptember-2013/show-and-tell-inside-ashley -murphys-dance-bag.

Garrett, Giannella. "Defying Gravity: Teen Ballerina Michaela DePrince." *TeenVogue.com*, May 2012. www.teenvogue.com /my-life/profiles/2012-05/teen-ballerina-michaela-deprince.

Gold, Sylviane. "Gwen Verdon." *Role Models*, November 2010, 12.

Harss, Marina. "Mesmerizing Moves." *Dance Magazine*, August 2013, 26–30.

Hayes, Hannah Maria. "Carrying the Jazz Torch." *Dance Teacher*, September 2010, 58–62.

Hecht, Elena. "Technique My Way: Julia Burrer." *Dance Magazine*, May 2013, 50.

"Hip hop." *Wikipedia*. Accessed July 10, 2013. en.wikipedia.org /wiki/Hip_hop.

Holleran, Leslie. "Angela Sterling: Ballet Photographer." *Beyond Performance*, September 2013, 4.

Holleran, Leslie. "Igor Stravinsky." *Dance Teacher*, September 2012, 78–80.

Holleran, Leslie. "Keeping Merce's Legacy Alive." *Dance Teacher*, December 2011, 20.

Hunt, Mary Ellen. "The Next Step." *Dance Magazine*, August 2013, 48–49.

"The Incredible Story of Ballerina Who Beat All the Odds to Become the First African American to Perform Solo in New York for 20 Years." *Daily Mail* website. June 2, 2013. www.daily mail.co.uk/news/article-2334929/Misty-Copland-Ballerina -African-American-perform-solo-New-York-20-YEARS.html.

Jones Donatelli, Jen. "Into the Great Wide Open." *Dance Teacher*, October 2011, 74–78.

Jones Donatelli, Jen. "Lyrcal Out Loud." *Dance Teacher*, December 2012, 39–42.

Jones, Tess. "Summer Cross Training." *Dance Teacher*, May 2013, 52–54.

"José Limón Dance Foundation." LinkedIn page. Accessed August 28, 3013. www.linkedin.com/company/2322483?trk =tyah&trkInfo=tarId%3A1397174178473%2Ctas%3Ajose%20 limon%20da%2Cidx%3A1-1-1.

Kasper, Courtney Rae. "Pyotr Ilyich Tchaikovsky." *Dance Teacher*, December 2011, 54.

Kaufman, Sarah. "2010 Pulitzer Prize: Sarah Kaufman on Winning Criticism, Role of Arts Coverage." *The Washington Post*, April 13, 2010. www.washingtonpost.com/wp-dyn /content/discussion/2010/04/13/DI2010041303523.html.

Kay, Lauren. "Centerwork: Not the Old Razzle Dazzle." *Dance Magazine*, May 2013, 46–48.

Kay, Lauren. "Jennifer Paulson Lee: Entrepreneur." *Beyond Performance*, September 2012, 10.

Kay, Lauren. "Making It Happen: College Goes Commercial." *Dance Magazine*, August 2013, 50–51.

Kay, Lauren. "Nathaniel Hathaway: Broadway Wig Supervisor." *Beyond Performance*, September 2013, 18.

Kay, Lauren. "Technique My Way: Ray Mercer." *Dance Magazine*, August 2013, 52–53.

Kourlas, Gia. "Where Are All the Black Swans?" *The New York Times*, May 6, 2007. www.nytimes.com/2007/05/06/arts /dance/06kour.html?pagewanted=all&_r=0.

"Lester Horton Dance Theater. DLC." SNAC: The Social Networks and Archival Context Project website. Accessed July 22, 2013. socialarchive.iath.virginia.edu/xtf/view?docId =lester-horton-dance-theater-cr.xml.

Levine, Debra. "Dance Theatre of Harlem's Tights of Another Color." *Los Angeles Times*, May 26, 2010. latimesblogs.latimes.com/culturemonster/2010/05/dance-theatre-of-harlems-tights-of-another-color.html.

Levine, Debra. "Talking with Dance Theatre of Harlem's Co-Founder Arthur Mitchell." *Los Angeles Times*, July 6, 2010. latimesblogs.latimes.com/culturemonster/2010/07/talking-with-dance-theatre-of-harlems-legendary-dancer-arthur-mitchell.html.

"Luvabulls 2012–13 Tryouts Information Sheet." The Official Site of the Chicago Bulls. Accessed January 16, 2014. blogs.bulls.com/wp-content/uploads/2012/06/luvabulls_packet_2012.pdf.

Macauley, Alastair. "Stories Told with a Twirl Here and a Leap There." *The New York Times*, August 13, 2013. www.nytimes.com/2013/08/14/arts/dance/downtown-dance-festival-dots-lower-manhattan.html.

Macias, Romy. "First African-American Ballerinas." Classical Ballet News website. March 15, 2012. classicalballetnews.com/first-african-american-ballerinas/.

McGuire, Kathleen. "The Good, the Bad, and the Ugly." *Dance Teacher*, October 2011, 92–94.

McGuire, Kathleen. "A Touchy Subject." *Dance Teacher*, October 2012, 94–96.

Murray, Rheana. "Teen Michaela DePrince Goes from War Orphan to Star Ballerina." *New York Daily News*. April 11, 2013. http://www.nydailynews.com/life-style/michaela-deprince-war-orphan-star-ballerina-article-1.1314010.

Naima. "Misty Copeland on Being Ballerina, Black and 'Curvy.'" PostBourgie, March 22, 2012. www.postbourgie.com/2011/03/22/misty-copeland-on-being-ballerina-black-and-curvy/.

Noveck, Jocelyn. "David Hallberg: How He Went from South Dakota to the Bolshoi." *The Huffington Post*, November 3, 2011. www.huffingtonpost.com/2011/11/03/david-hallberg-bolshoi_n_1073380.html.

Poon, Kina. "The Sublime Hee Seo." *Dance Magazine*, May 2013, 24–28.

Pressley, Nelson. "Kathleen Marshall, Broadway's 'Vintage Girl.'" *The Washington Post*, June 7, 2013. www.washingtonpost.com /entertainment/theater_dance/kathleen-marshall-broadways -vintage-girl/2013/06/06/1aee2bcc-cc99-11e2-8573 -3baeea6a2647_story.html.

Prevots, Naime. "Lester Horton (1906–1953)." *NYC Dance Stuff* (blog). September 22, 2012. nycdancestuff.wordpress.com /2012/09/22/lester-horton-1906-1953-by-naima-prevots/.

Rizzuto, Rachel. "Bill 'Bojangles' Robinson." *Dance Teacher*, May 2013, 56–58.

Rolnick, Katie. "Fine, All Right, Cool." *Dance Teacher*, December 2012, 64–65.

Rolnick, Katie. "Gregory Hines." *Dance Teacher*, May 2010, 56–58.

"Ruth St. Denis." Jacob's Pillow Dance website. Accessed July 27, 2013. www.jacobspillow.org/exhibits-archives/artist -profiles/ruth-st-denis/.

Schwab, Kristin. "Extra Credit." *Dance Teacher*, January 2012, 52–54.

Schwab, Kristin. "Face to Face: From the Heartland to the Orient." *Dance Teacher*, January 2012, 22.

Schwab, Kristin. "The Great Debate." *Dance Teacher*, May 2013, 62–64.

Seidman, Mary. "Architects of Body and Soul." *Dance Teacher*, September 2010, 46–45.

Stahl, Jennifer. "Back in the Studio." *Secrets of a Successful Studio* supplement, September 2012, 20.

Strauss, Rachel. "He's the One." *Dance Teacher*, October 2011, 96–98.

Strauss, Rachel. "Isadora Duncan." *Dance Teacher*, January 2012, 44–46.

"Stephen Boss." The Internet Movie Database. Accessed April 11, 2014. imdb.com/name/nm2798774/.

Sucato, Steve. "Marisa Cerveris: Dancewear Designer." *Beyond Performance*, September 2010, 18.

Tarnay, Linda. " Robert Small: Landscape Designer." *Beyond Performance*, September 2011, 20.

Trueman, Matt. "Misty Copeland Raises Bar for Black Ballet Dancers." *The Guardian*, June 4, 2013. www.theguardian.com /stage/2013/jun/04/misty-copeland-black-ballet-dancer.

Turan, Kenneth. "Children in Love with Ballet in 'First Position.'" *Los Angeles Times*, May 4, 2012. articles.latimes.com/2012 /may/04/entertainment/la-et-first-position-20120504.

Whitney, Barbara. "William Forsythe." Encyclopedia Britannica. Accessed August 1, 2013. www.britannica.com/EBchecked /topic/1090933/William-Forsythe.

Wozny, Nancy. "10 Common Dance Injuries." *Dance Teacher*, August 2010, 72–73.

Yung, Susan. "Dance Matters: Stretching Her Wings." *Dance Magazine*, August 2013, 18.

Zar, Rachel. "Larissa Saveliev's Solo Suggestions for Your Battle Students." *Dance Teacher*, December 2011, 24.

Books

Barringer, Janice and Sarah Schlesinger. *The Pointe Book, Revised Edition.* Hightstown, NJ: Princeton Book Company, 1998.

Chang, Jeff. *Can't Stop Won't Stop: A History of the Hip-Hop Generation.* New York: Picador, 2005.

Clarke, Mary and Clement Crisp. *The History of Dance.* New York: Crown Publishers, 1981.

Conrad, Christine. *Jerome Robbins: That Broadway Man, That Ballet Man.* London: Booth-Cibborn, 2000.

Copeland, Misty. *Life in Motion: An Unlikely Ballerina.* New York: Simon & Schuster, 2014.

Dagenais, Mande. *Starting Your Career as a Dancer.* New York: Allworth Press, 2012.

Gilvey, John Anthony. *Before the Parade Passes By: Gower Champion and the Glorious American Musical.* New York: St. Martin's Press, 2005.

Gottried, Martin. *All His Jazz: The Life and Death of Bob Fosse.* New York: Bantam Books, 1990.

Graham, Martha. *Blood Memory.* New York: Doubleday, 1991.

Greene Haas, Jacqi. *Dance Anatomy.* Champaign, IL: Human Kinetics, 2010.

Hoffman, Jennifer. *Apollo's Angels.* New York: Random House, 2010.

Kirkland, Gelsey and Greg Lawrence. *Dancing on My Grave.* New York: Doubleday & Company, 1986.

Kislan, Richard. *Hoofing It on Broadway: A History of Show Dancing.* New York: Prentice Hall, 1987.

Reich, Susanna. *José: Born to Dance.* New York: Simon & Schuster, 2005.

Reyna, Ferdinando. *A Concise History of Ballet.* New York: Grosset & Dunlap, 1965.

Schumacher, Thomas and Jeff Kurtti. *How Does the Show Go On: An Introduction to the Theater.* New York: Disney Editions, 2007.

Sennet, Ted. *Hollywood Musicals*. New York: Harry N. Abrams, 1981.

Sharp, Adrienne. *The True Memoirs of Little K*. New York: Farrar, Strauss & Giroux, 2010.

Terry, Walter. *Miss Ruth: The "More Living Life" of Ruth St. Denis*. New York: Dodd, Mead & Company, 1969.

Vagonova, Agrippina. *Basic Principles of Classical Ballet: Russian Ballet Technique*. New York: Dover Publications, 1969.

Websites

Alvin Ailey American Dance Theater, alvinailey.org

American Association of Community Theatre:

 artistic director, aact.org/people/artistic.html

 chief administrative officer, aact.org/people/chiefadmin.html

 marketing/publicity, aact.org/people/publicity.html

 production manager/producer, aact.org/people/Producer.html

 stage manager, aact.org/people/stagemanager.html

 technical director, aact.org/people/techdirector.html

American Ballet Theatre, abt.org

American Theatre Wing, americantheatrewing.org

Backstage, backstage.com

Ballet Black, balletblack.co.uk

Ballet Hispanico, ballethispanico.org

Body Traffic, bodytraffic.com

Boston Ballet, bostonballet.org

Broadway Dance Center, broadwaydancecenter.com

Broadway: The American Musical, pbs.org/wnet/broadway

Complexions Contemporary Ballet, complexionsdance.org

Central Pennsylvania Youth Ballet, cpyb.org

Dance Heritage Coalition, danceheritage.org

Dance Theatre of Harlem, dancetheatreofharlem.org

Dance U101, danceu101.com

David Hallberg, davidhallberg.com

The Forsythe Company, theforsythecompany.com

Houston Ballet, houstonballet.org

Hubbard Street Dance Chicago, hubbardstreetdance.com

Jerome Robbins, jeromerobbins.org

Joffrey Ballet, joffrey.com

José Limón Dance Company, limon.org

Masterworks Broadway, masterworks.com

Martha Graham, marthagraham.org

Michaela DePrince, michaeladeprince.com

Millennium Dance Complex, millenniumdancecomplex.com

New York City Ballet, nycballet.com

Paul Taylor Dance Company, ptdc.org

Portland Dancing, portlanddancing.com

Twyla Tharp, twylatharp.org